S0-ARM-941

making
a movie in
iMovie and iDVD

Visual QuickProject Guide

by Jeff Carlson

**Peachpit
Press**

Visual QuickProject Guide
Making a Movie in iMovie and iDVD
Jeff Carlson

Peachpit Press
1249 Eighth Street
Berkeley, CA 94710
510/524-2178
800/283-9444
510/524-2221 (fax)

Find us on the World Wide Web at: www.peachpit.com
To report errors, please send a note to errata@peachpit.com
Peachpit Press is a division of Pearson Education

Copyright © 2005 by Jeff Carlson

Editor: Nancy Davis
Production editor: Lisa Brazieal, Myrna Vladic
Copy editor: Liane Thomas
Compositor: Jeff Carlson
Indexer: Caroline Parks
Cover design: The Visual Group with Aren Howell
Interior design: Elizabeth Castro

Notice of Rights
All rights reserved. No part of this book may be reproduced or transmitted in any form by any means, electronic, mechanical, photocopying, recording, or otherwise, without the prior written permission of the publisher. For information on getting permission for reprints and excerpts, contact permissions@peachpit.com.

Notice of Liability
The information in this book is distributed on an "As Is" basis, without warranty. While every precaution has been taken in the preparation of the book, neither the author nor Peachpit Press shall have any liability to any person or entity with respect to any loss or damage caused or alleged to be caused directly or indirectly by the instructions contained in this book or by the computer software and hardware products described in it.

Trademarks
Visual QuickProject Guide is a registered trademark of Peachpit Press, a division of Pearson Education.
iMovie, iDVD, iTunes, iLife, iPhoto, and GarageBand are trademarks or registered trademarks of Apple Computer, Inc., registered in the United States and other countries. All other trademarks are the property of their respective owners. Throughout this book, trademarks are used. Rather than put a trademark symbol with every occurrence of a trademarked name, we state that we are using the names in an editorial fashion only and to the benefit of the trademark owner with no intention of infringement of the trademark. No such use, or the use of any trade name, is intended to convey endorsement or other affiliation with this book.

ISBN 0-321-27846-1

9 8 7 6 5 4 3 2

Printed and bound in the United States of America

For Janet and Linda

Special Thanks to...

Kimberly for her ceaseless love and support, and for taking me to Arizona in the first place;

Janet and Linda for being excellent tour guides;

Lisa Brazieal for assistance in producing the book and listening to my layout ideas;

Liane Thomas for being the sharp eyes of this book, even while chatting via iChat at 2 a.m.;

Caroline Parks for indexing the book in record time;

Everyone at Peachpit Press for helping me enjoy what I do for a living;

My officemates Glenn, Jeff, Agen, Larry, and Kim for encouragement and conversation;

Diva Espresso for delicious consciousness in a cup (or two, or dozens);

and to Nancy Davis: I don't know how you do it all, but I'm glad that you do.

contents

contents

contents

contents

introduction

The Visual QuickProject Guide that you hold in your hands offers a unique way to learn about new technologies. Instead of drowning you in theoretical possibilities and lengthy explanations, this Visual QuickProject Guide uses big, color illustrations coupled with clear, concise step-by-step instructions to show you how to complete one specific project in a matter of hours.

Our project in this book is to edit a home movie and put it on a DVD that can be viewed using most consumer DVD players. Why go to the trouble of editing? After all, the footage shot on the camcorder's tape is a movie—all the pieces are there, and can be played back from start to end. However, the video you shoot invariably includes rough patches that always crop up: blurry shots when you were trying to locate something in the viewfinder; sections of time when the camera was inadvertently recording the ground as you were walking; and, for lack of a polite way of saying it, those parts that seemed interesting at the time but on reflection are now just boring.

With iMovie, you will take that footage and easily shape it into a movie that your friends and family want to watch. In addition to assembling and trimming scenes, you'll add music, sound effects, and still photos. Once the movie is edited, you'll be able to post it on the Web, send it to someone via email, and burn it to a DVD using iDVD. What's great is that you don't have to be a professional video editor or even a computer expert to accomplish this task.

what you'll create

Import your video footage from a digital camcorder into iMovie.

Add photos from iPhoto, with the Ken Burns Effect applied to create a sense of motion in the still images.

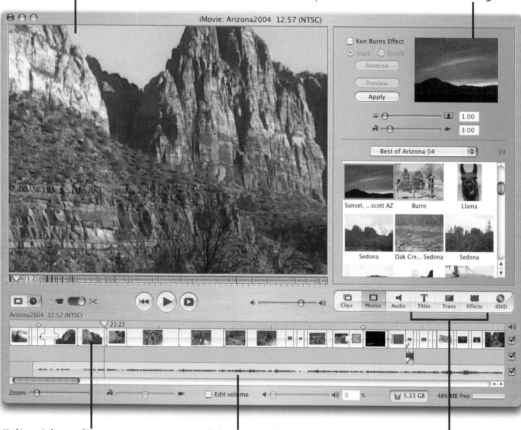

Edit video clips to tighten the action, eliminate boring parts, and tell a story.

Add music from iTunes to play in the background.

Create titles, transitions, and effects to produce a more professional-looking movie.

Create a project in iDVD that includes the movie you edited in iMovie.

Increase visual interest by adding a movie or photos to a drop zone.

Choose one of 58 attractive, motion-enabled themes for your DVD's menu.

Customize the appearance of navigation buttons based on your movies and photos.

Create submenus that contain more content, such as video or slideshows built from iPhoto.

Burn a DVD-R disc of your project that can be played in consumer DVD players.

how this book works

The title of each section explains what is covered on that page.

Numbered steps explain actions to perform in a specific order.

Important terms and Web site addresses are shown in orange.

A dotted arrow indicates movement you need to make, such as dragging an object to an area of the interface.

Captions explain what you're doing and why. They also point to relevant sections of the interface.

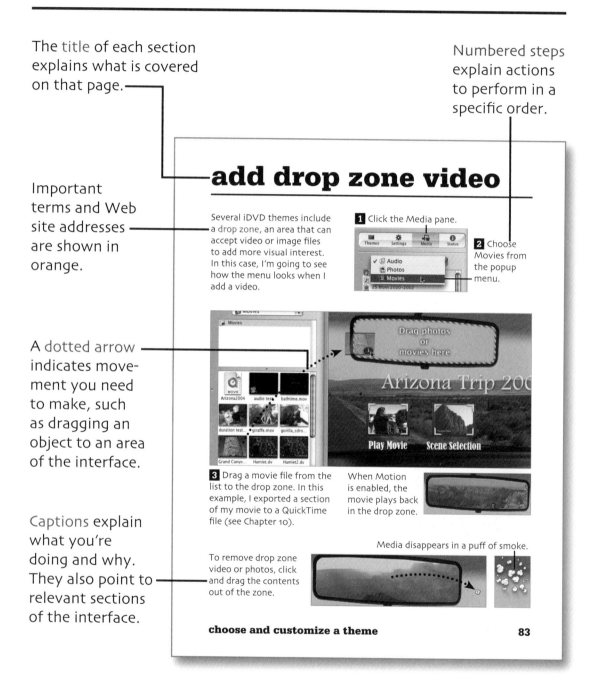

add drop zone video

Several iDVD themes include a drop zone, an area that can accept video or image files to add more visual interest. In this case, I'm going to see how the menu looks when I add a video.

1 Click the Media pane.

2 Choose Movies from the popup menu.

3 Drag a movie file from the list to the drop zone. In this example, I exported a section of my movie to a QuickTime file (see Chapter 10).

When Motion is enabled, the movie plays back in the drop zone.

Media disappears in a puff of smoke.

To remove drop zone video or photos, click and drag the contents out of the zone.

choose and customize a theme

83

The extra bits section at the end of each chapter contains additional tips and tricks that you might like to know—but that aren't absolutely necessary.

add drop zone video

The heading for each group of tips matches the section title.

extra bits

apply a theme   p. 78
- If 58 built-in themes aren't enough for you, consider buying themes from third-party developers. See Appendix B for more information.
- Some themes include background music when the Motion button is enabled. That's fine for playing the DVD on a television, but can be grating while editing. I usually activate motion only when I need to view an animated element.

edit the title   p. 79
When using Custom position for the title, remember that most television screens cut off part of the visible image. Choose Show TV Safe Area from the Advanced menu to view recommended boundaries.

edit the buttons   p. 80
To make multiple-line button titles, simply hit Return between words.

edit motion buttons   p. 82
Is nothing happening when you click the Motion button? Go to the Settings pane, and check the Duration slider—it may have gotten set to zero. Duration controls how much of the menu's motion plays before starting over. Typically, this amount is the menu's longest background movie or audio, but you can set it lower.

add drop zone video   p. 83
- If you'd rather not see the drop zone text ("Drag photos…"), go to iDVD's preferences and uncheck Show Drop Zones. The zones are still there, just not explicitly marked.
- You can also drag video files from the Finder to a drop zone, instead of using the Media pane.
- A drop zone video plays back from the beginning of the clip; you can't choose a starting frame the way you can with motion buttons.

The page number next to the heading makes it easy to refer back to the main content.

choose and customize a theme   89

the web site

Find this book's companion Web site at
http://www.necoffee.com/imovievqs/

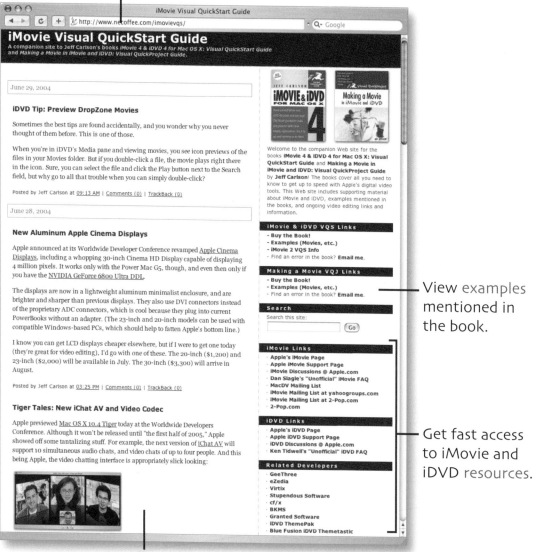

View examples mentioned in the book.

Get fast access to iMovie and iDVD resources.

Stay current with iMovie, iDVD, and iLife-related news, tips, and opinions, updated regularly.

the next step

While this Visual QuickProject Guide will walk you through all of the steps required to edit a movie and burn it to a DVD, there's more to learn about iMovie and iDVD. After you complete your QuickProject, consider picking up my book iMovie 4 & iDVD 4 for Mac OS X: Visual QuickStart Guide as an in-depth, handy reference.

The book includes information on using expert settings when exporting QuickTime movies, using GarageBand to score background music, shortcuts for working in the Timeline, and more. It also features a whole section on the basics of video editing, including using camcorders, composing shots, moving the camera, lighting scenes, and capturing audio.

1. project overview

You can shoot and edit all kinds of movies: wedding videos, fictional stories, scripted documentaries, sporting events, or just in-the-moment scenes of babies, pets, land-scapes, clouds…your only true limits are the amount of tape and the camcorder's battery life. For this Visual QuickProject Guide, I'm creating a vacation video from a recent trip to Arizona. Nearly every task I show in this book applies to other types of movies, so don't worry if the movie you're editing isn't a vacation video. Then again, if you've been itching to go on a vacation anyway, maybe this is a good excuse to get out there and capture your own footage!

project overview

Here's what you'll be able to do by the end of the book:

1 Import the video footage from a digital camcorder into iMovie (see Chapter 3).

2 Assemble the movie by choosing the order of the video clips, adding audio, and importing some digital still photos (see Chapters 4–5).

3 Edit the clips to remove footage you don't need and improve the movie's timing and flow (see Chapter 6).

4 Add titles, transitions, and effects to the movie (see Chapters 7–9).

5 Share the movie with others by creating a QuickTime version that can be burned to a CD-ROM or uploaded to a Web site, such as an Apple .Mac HomePage (see Chapter 10).

6 Create an iDVD project that contains your movie (also in Chapter 10).

7 Edit the project in iDVD by choosing a new menu theme and personalizing its appearance (see Chapters 11-12).

8 Add more media to the DVD, such as other QuickTime movies and a slideshow of some of your digital still photos, which can be viewed separately from your main movie (see Chapters 13).

9 Burn the project to a DVD disc that can be played back in most consumer DVD players and DVD-equipped computers (see Chapter 14).

Editing video in iMovie, and creating DVDs in iDVD, is fun, easy, and even slightly addictive. With this initial project under your belt, you'll be ready to tackle others on your own.

project materials

A Macintosh computer (desktop or laptop) with a PowerPC G3, G4, or G5 processor running at 300 MHz or faster. iMovie 4 and iDVD 4 require Mac OS X 10.2.6 or later.

At least 10 GB of free space on your hard drive.

A built-in Super-Drive if you plan on burning DVDs.

iMovie

iDVD

A digital camcorder and MiniDV tapes for shooting video footage.

4-pin to 6-pin FireWire cable to connect the camcorder to the Mac.

Blank DVD-R discs (if your Mac contains a SuperDrive and you want to burn DVDs).

iMovie 4.0.1 or later, and iDVD 4.0.1 or later (part of the iLife '04 package).

movie editing overview

1 Shoot Video. Go into the wild (or just into the living room) to capture the video footage that you will later edit in iMovie.

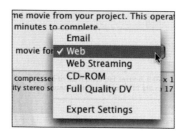

2 Import Footage into iMovie. Use iMovie's Import feature to save the footage to your hard disk as clips.

3 Assemble Your Movie. Drag movie clips to the Timeline to determine their order of appearance. Also, add audio (such as music or sound effects), digital still photos, or other content that appears in the movie.

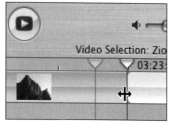

4 Edit Clips. With a rough version of your movie in place, edit the individual clips to remove unwanted frames, trim clips for timing, and add transitions, titles, and effects. This is the polishing stage, where the movie really comes together.

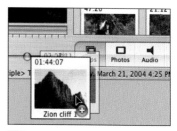

5 Share Your Movie. It's done! Now, save the movie out of iMovie into a format that other people can view, such as a QuickTime file, .Mac HomePage, or iDVD project.

dvd creation overview

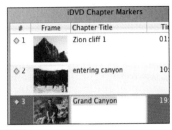

1 Prepare in iMovie. Create iDVD Chapter Markers in iMovie to access individual chapters within the movie when you play the DVD.

2 Create iDVD Project. The easiest way to move from iMovie to iDVD is to use the Create iDVD Project command. iMovie prepares the data, launches iDVD, and saves a new iDVD project containing your movie.

3 Edit the DVD Theme. Each DVD menu has a visual theme that not only makes it attractive, but provides links and folders to your movie and other content. Choose one of iDVD's existing themes and then customize its appearance.

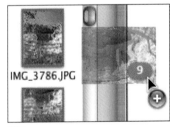

4 Add Other Content. Your DVD can include just your movie, but if there's enough room on the disc, you can add QuickTime movies, photo slideshows, and other data.

5 Burn the DVD Disc. Time to etch your project into a disc's surface. Choose the type of encoding, double-check that everything is set, and then burn the disc in a SuperDrive.

2. create an iMovie project

1 Double-click the iMovie icon in your Applications folder. If the iLife '04 installer placed iMovie onto the Dock, you can also single-click it there.

On your hard disk, the project folder includes the project file (which ends in .iMovieProj), and a Media folder where all the imported video is stored.

2 This dialog appears the first time you launch iMovie. Click the Create Project button. (If you've ever previously opened iMovie, the last active project opens automatically.)

3 In the Save dialog that appears, type a name for your project and choose a location to store it on your hard disk.

iMovie's interface

The Monitor is where you preview and edit clips and play back the entire movie.

The Shelf (also known as the Clips pane) is a virtual storage area where all your video clips are held before being added to the movie. This is also where other panes, such as Titles and Transitions, appear.

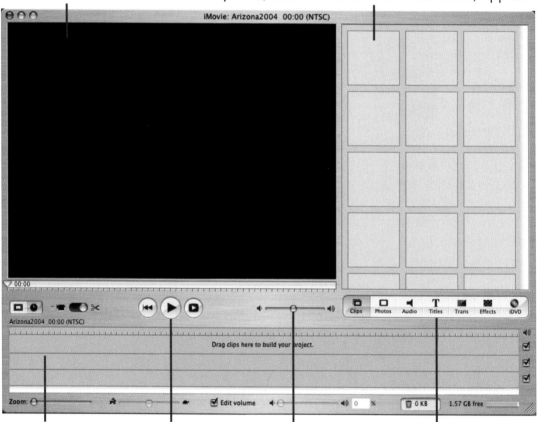

Assemble your clips in the Liquid Timeline, placing them left to right in the order you want them to play.

The playback controls jump to the beginning of the movie, play the movie in real time, or play the movie in full-screen mode.

The Volume slider controls the volume of movie playback. It doesn't affect the volume level of individual clips, however.

The buttons below the shelf access panes that control features such as creating titles and accessing photos.

create an iMovie project

the Liquid Timeline

The Liquid Timeline (so named because of the slick visual morph that occurs when you switch between timeline modes) uses two ways to work with your clips: the Clip Viewer and the Timeline Viewer.

Clip Viewer button

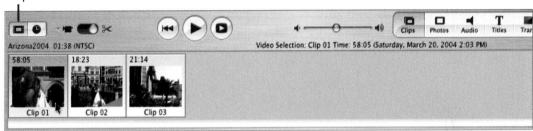

Click the Clip Viewer button (or press ⌘-E) to display the Clip Viewer component of the Liquid Timeline. In this mode, clips appear as thumbnails of the same size, which can be rearranged by dragging them (see Chapter 4).

Timeline Viewer button   Video track   Audio track 1   Audio track 2

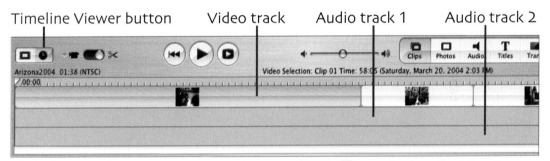

Click the Timeline Viewer button (or press ⌘-E) to display the Timeline Viewer. This mode displays clips sized according to their duration. The Timeline Viewer also includes two audio tracks below the video track for adding audio files (see Chapter 5). This is the component you will use most when trimming clips and editing audio.

As you'll see in Chapters 6-9, you can use both Viewers to add and delete clips, titles, transitions, and effects.

extra bits

create an iMovie project p. 7

- Remember to save your project often. Choose Save from the File menu, or press ⌘-S. In the unfortunate (but possible) event that iMovie crashes, you'd lose any changes made since the last time you saved the project. Trust me, I've been burned by this too many times in the past; now I think of myself as a serial saver.

- You don't have to save your project into your Home folder. When you create a new project, feel free to save it anywhere on your hard disk.

- When I'm working on a project, I usually save it to either an external FireWire hard drive (you can get 80 GB models now for around $100), or to a partition on my computer's hard disk where I keep some works in progress. A partition is basically a section of your hard disk that appears on the desktop as if it were a completely different volume. (If you want to partition a drive, use Apple's Disk Utility application. Be sure to back up all of your data, because partitioning a drive erases it first!)

Why use a partition or external hard disk? In addition to providing more storage, it's disk space that won't get as fragmented (i.e., pieces of data are written to lots of different areas on the disk). When data is fragmented, it takes longer for the drive to locate the data—granted, it's usually a matter of milliseconds, but if a drive is severely fragmented, iMovie can drop frames and otherwise not behave nicely.

- Mac OS X 10.3 Panther includes a feature called FileVault, which promises to increase the security of your data by encrypting the contents of your Home folder. Unfortunately, that's where Apple's programs store video files, iTunes music, and other large files. If you're running an iMovie project stored in the Home folder and have FileVault enabled, every byte that iMovie uses must be decrypted on the fly. The result is poor performance and potentially bad data loss. I really like the idea of FileVault, but its current incarnation is just too poorly implemented for real-world use.

- When you close a project, iMovie quits. Only one iMovie project can be open at a time.

3. import video into iMovie

Although the video footage captured by your digital camcorder is recorded as long series of ones and zeros, it's written on magnetic tape (which is still the best way to store the vast amount of information that digital video occupies). To turn that footage into a malleable form that you can edit, you need to bring it from the camera's tape to your hard disk. iMovie calls this importing.

Before you start, make sure you have plenty of free space on your hard disk: importing a typical 60-minute MiniDV tape takes up roughly 13 gigabytes (GB) of hard disk space.

Here's the math, if you're curious:

1 second of video equals 3.6 MB.

3.6 MB x 60 seconds = 216 MB per minute.

216 MB x 60 minutes = 12,960 MB.

connect the camcorder

6-pin to 4-pin FireWire cable

Power switch

DV port

1 Connect the FireWire cable to the camcorder and your Mac.

2 Switch the camcorder to Play/ VCR mode (the name can vary among camera manufacturers).

3 Launch iMovie. It should go into Camera mode automatically; if not, click the mode switch to change from Edit mode to Camera mode.

Edit mode

Camera mode

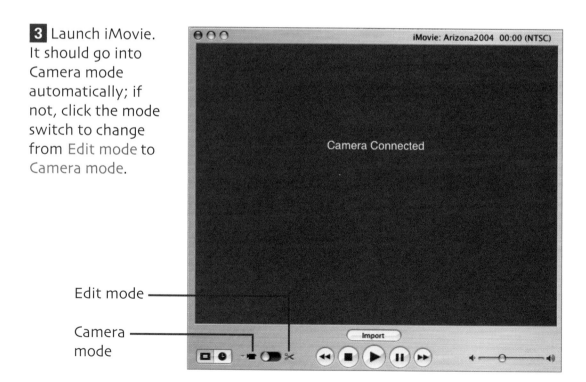

import video into iMovie

review your footage

When the camera is connected, you can use iMovie's controls to rewind, fast-forward, and play through the footage on tape. This lets you locate footage without fiddling with the camera's miniscule buttons. If nothing else, I find it easier to rewind the tape using iMovie.

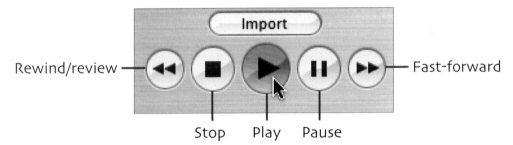

Rewind/review   Fast-forward

Stop   Play   Pause

Press Rewind or Fast-forward while the video is playing to review the footage sped up.

import your footage

Here's the (not so) hard part: click the Import button to start importing your footage. iMovie automatically starts playback on the camcorder.

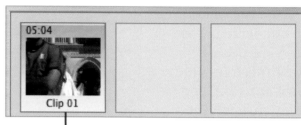

Footage appears on the Shelf as a clip.

As you import, iMovie identifies the moments in your footage when you stopped recording one scene and started recording the next. When such a break is encountered, iMovie creates a new clip for each scene.

New clip created for next scene.

After importing the clips you want (the entire tape, in this case), click the Import button again to stop.

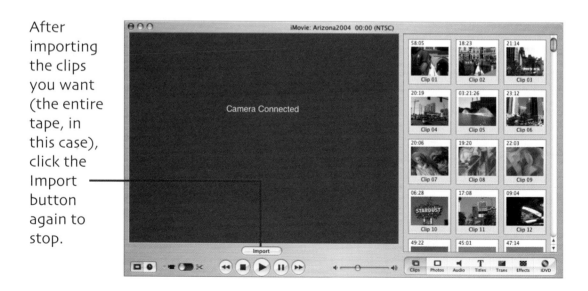

import video into iMovie

timecode

Now that your footage is in iMovie, you need to become familiar with the way video is measured: timecode. A movie is made up of thousands of frames, so clips are measured in terms of minutes, seconds, and frames. In video, 30 frames equals 1 second; so, for example, a timecode value of 10:15 is ten and a half seconds.

For short clips, iMovie displays only the seconds and frames, (since 00:10:15 is presumably a waste of space). If you would prefer the longer notation, go to iMovie's preferences and uncheck the "Display short time codes" option.

As you start working with clips, timecode will soon become second nature.

Length of clip in timecode: 23 seconds and 14 frames

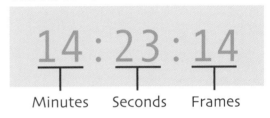

Timecode notation

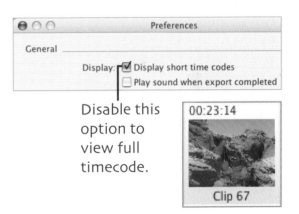

Disable this option to view full timecode.

extra bits

connect the camcorder p. 12

- Quit other applications before importing to make sure that their actions in the background (such as checking email, playing music, etc.) don't interfere with the import process. Otherwise, you could encounter dropped frames or stuttery playback.

- If you have an iSight that's connected at the same time as your camcorder, and you want to capture live video with it, click the camera icon next to the mode switch and choose iSight from the popup menu that appears.

review your footage p. 13

If you're importing sections of your tape (instead of the entire tape), rewind to a few seconds before the start of what you want to capture. This gives you some buffer later on while editing (see Chapter 6).

import your footage p. 14

- Press the spacebar in Camera mode to start importing footage. Press it again to stop.

- The free space indicator in the lower-right corner of iMovie's window keeps tabs on how much room is left on your hard disk. As the disk fills up, the indicator changes from green to yellow to red. When no more space is free, iMovie stops the import process.

- You can also import QuickTime movies from your hard disk. Simply drag the QuickTime file from the Finder onto the Shelf. However, since most QuickTime movies are smaller in size, the resolution may not be as good as your camcorder's footage.

- You can buy analog-to-digital converter boxes, which enable you to connect an analog camcorder or VCR to your Mac and import that footage into iMovie. I used one recently to digitize and edit the video from my wedding, since VHS tapes noticeably deteriorate.

- If, as you import, you hear an echo, check your camera's volume level. If it's audible, you'll hear the footage's audio first from the camcorder's speakers, and then from your Mac's speakers a fraction of a second after.

import video into iMovie

4. assemble your movie

Your footage is now in iMovie, but you don't have a movie quite yet. To borrow from another art form, your project is now a block of marble just waiting for the chisel that will reveal the statue within. And like a sculptor, you need to reveal your movie gradually, creating a rough shape before refining the details. In this chapter, you'll move your clips from the Shelf to the Liquid Timeline and put them in order.

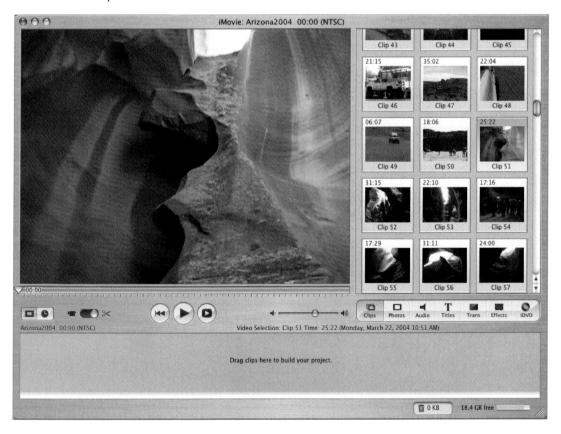

add clips to timeline

It may not be high-tech, but I find it essential to make a quick outline of the movie's high points to use as a road map.

I also spend some time renaming significant clips to help identify them while editing.

Click once on the clip's name to edit.

Highlight the current name.

Type a new name, and press Return.

1 Click the Clip Viewer button to display that mode of the Liquid Time-line.

2 Drag one or more clips from the Shelf to the Clip Viewer. Congratulations, you've just made a (rough) movie!

assemble your movie

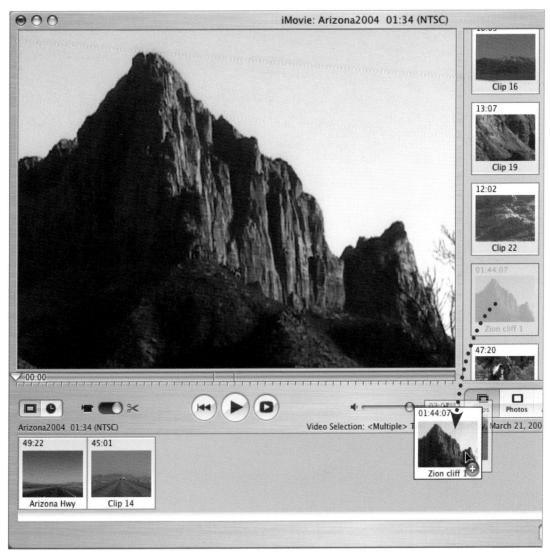

3 Continue to drag the clips you want to use into the Clip Viewer. Don't worry about the order that they're in—your goal at this point is to put together a rough assembly of the raw materials you'll be working with. Any clip added to the Clip Viewer becomes part of your movie.

arrange the clips

iMovie is nonlinear: you can arrange clips in any order you wish.
Reposition clips in the Clip Viewer to determine the order they will play.

1 Click and hold on a clip to select it.

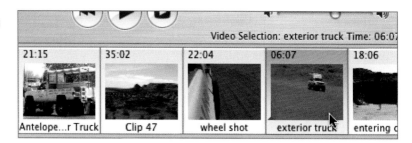

2 Drag the clip to a new location in the Clip Viewer.

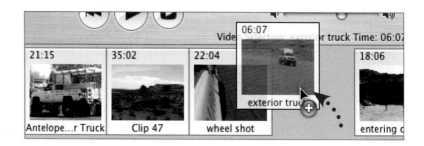

As you drag, other clips automatically slide out of the way of the selected clip.

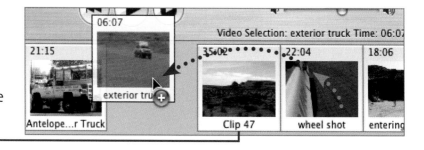

3 Release the mouse button where you want the clip to appear. It falls into place.

assemble your movie

As you're arranging your clips, use the Shelf as a convenient holding area. For example, I've found two clips that I know would be great as the beginning (where I will want to add my titles later) and closing scenes in the movie.

This cactus clip actually appeared at the end of the tape, so first I reposition it on the shelf for easy access...

...and then later drag it to the beginning of my timeline to appear as the first clip.

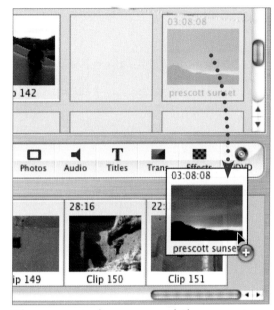

The sunset clip, meanwhile, goes to the end of the timeline.

If you absolutely don't need a clip, drag it to iMovie's Trash (or press the ⎉Delete⎉ key). However, do not empty the Trash while you're in the middle of an editing project (see the Extra Bits section at the end of this chapter). ──────

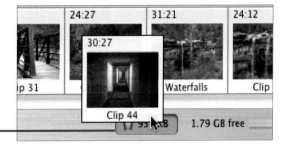

arrange the clips (continued)

With all of our clips added to the timeline, you can see that the total duration of our movie is just over 51 minutes! But that's okay, because as we start editing the individual clips, we'll soon trim the movie down closer to a goal of 10-15 minutes.

Drag the horizontal scroll bar
to view all of your clips.

extra bits

add clips to timeline p. 18

Don't empty the Trash! Unlike the Trash in the Finder, clips deleted in iMovie are tough to fish back out (though there are ways—see Chapter 6). If you empty the Trash, however, the clip is gone for good. Why? As you're editing, iMovie keeps track of which sections of your footage are being used, and which have been discarded...but the media files on your hard disk don't change. When you empty the Trash, however, iMovie rewrites the media files to remove trashed footage, permanently deleting the tossed scenes. The only way to retrieve the footage at that point is to re-import it from your camcorder.

arrange the clips p. 20

- The Clip Viewer is the only mode of the Liquid Timeline that allows you to rearrange clips. The Timeline Viewer is designed to edit clips, not move them.

- Although I've structured this book so that all the clips are added in this one stage of editing, you can drag clips in and out of the Clip Viewer at any time.

5. add photos and music

Even when I'm not on vacation, I usually have a digital still camera close at hand. A typical still camera captures more image resolution than a camcorder; plus, I like to send snapshots to friends and family.

Most camcorders sold today can also shoot still images, so you've no doubt accumulated a bunch of photos. If you use iPhoto to organize your pictures, you can easily grab them from within iMovie and add them to your movie. And with the Ken Burns Effect, you can add some pan and zoom effects to make the photos more interesting.

At this stage, it also helps to add background music to your movie (if you choose). Later, you can your edit clips so they're timed to your tunes.

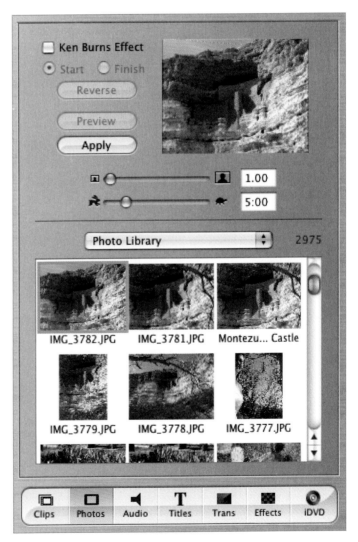

import photos

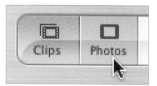

1 Switch to the Photos pane by clicking the Photos button.

2 Make sure the Ken Burns Effect is disabled (we'll cover that feature on page 28).

I created a new album in iPhoto for my vacation pictures. Choosing the album name from the popup menu displays only those photos.

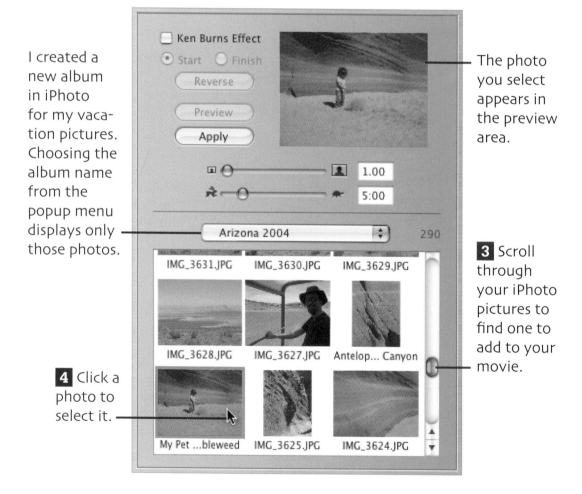

The photo you select appears in the preview area.

3 Scroll through your iPhoto pictures to find one to add to your movie.

4 Click a photo to select it.

add photos and music

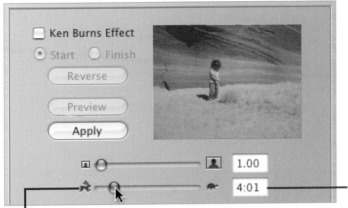

You can
also type
a new
time value
into the
Duration
field.

5 Move the Duration slider to specify how long the still photo will appear in the movie.

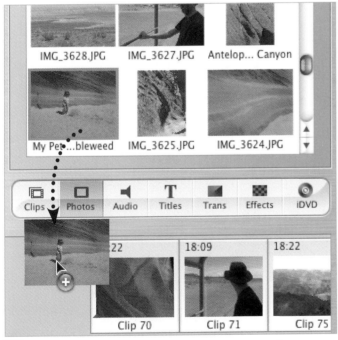

This icon indicates that a photo in the Clip Viewer isn't a normal video clip.

6 Drag the photo to the Clip Viewer (shown here) or Timeline Viewer to add it to your movie.

add photos and music

add motion to photos

The Ken Burns Effect (named after the documentary filmmaker who popularized the technique) adds motion to still pictures by panning and zooming—focusing on a portion of the image and moving the camera over it. To do so, set the appearance of the first frame of the effect (the Start), and then set the last frame (the Finish). iMovie then calculates the frames in-between to produce the effect. For this example, I want to start zoomed in on a photo of some handsome tourist, then zoom out to reveal the Grand Canyon.

1 Click here to enable the effect.

2 Click the Start button to set up the first frame of the effect.

3 Change the zoom amount by dragging the Zoom slider, or typing a value into the Zoom field.

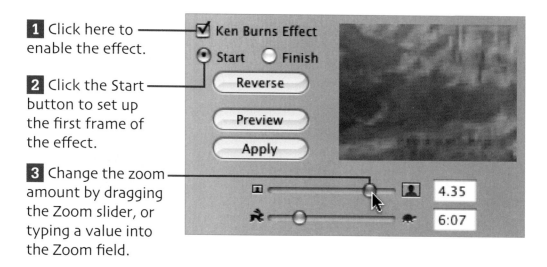

4 Click and drag in the preview area to locate the section of the image you want visible.

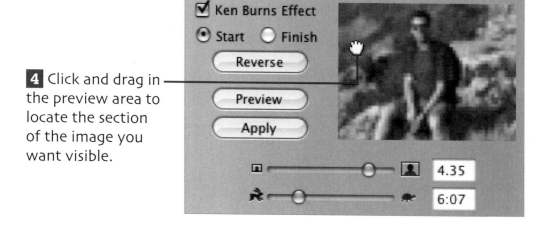

5 Click the Finish button to set up the last frame of the effect.

As you work, click here to preview the effect.

6 Change the zoom amount. In this case, I'm zooming almost entirely out.

☑ Ken Burns Effect
○ Start ◉ Finish
Reverse
Preview
Apply

1.02
6:07

7 Drag the image to the Timeline to add it to your movie.

Grand Canyon IMG_4672.JPG IMC

Clips • Photos Audio Titles Trans

18:22

Clip 75

06:07

Grand Canyon

iMovie renders the photo as a video clip; the red line indicates rendering progress.

The completed effect:
Start

Finish

add photos and music

add music from iTunes

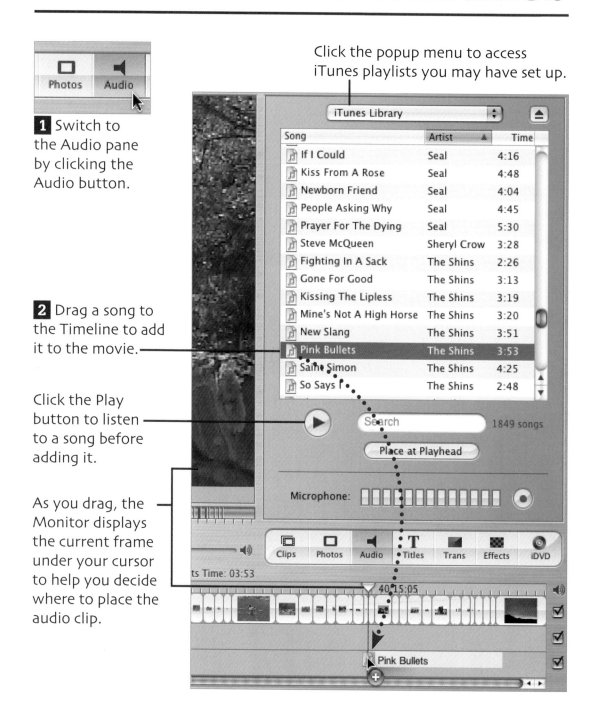

Switch to the Audio pane by clicking the Audio button.

Click the popup menu to access iTunes playlists you may have set up.

1 Switch to the Audio pane by clicking the Audio button.

2 Drag a song to the Timeline to add it to the movie.

Click the Play button to listen to a song before adding it.

As you drag, the Monitor displays the current frame under your cursor to help you decide where to place the audio clip.

iTunes Library

Song	Artist ▲	Time
If I Could	Seal	4:16
Kiss From A Rose	Seal	4:48
Newborn Friend	Seal	4:04
People Asking Why	Seal	4:45
Prayer For The Dying	Seal	5:30
Steve McQueen	Sheryl Crow	3:28
Fighting In A Sack	The Shins	2:26
Gone For Good	The Shins	3:13
Kissing The Lipless	The Shins	3:19
Mine's Not A High Horse	The Shins	3:20
New Slang	The Shins	3:51
Pink Bullets	The Shins	3:53
Saint Simon	The Shins	4:25
So Says I	The Shins	2:48

Search   1849 songs

Place at Playhead

Microphone:

Clips   Photos   Audio   Titles   Trans   Effects   iDVD

ts Time: 03:53   40:15:05

Pink Bullets

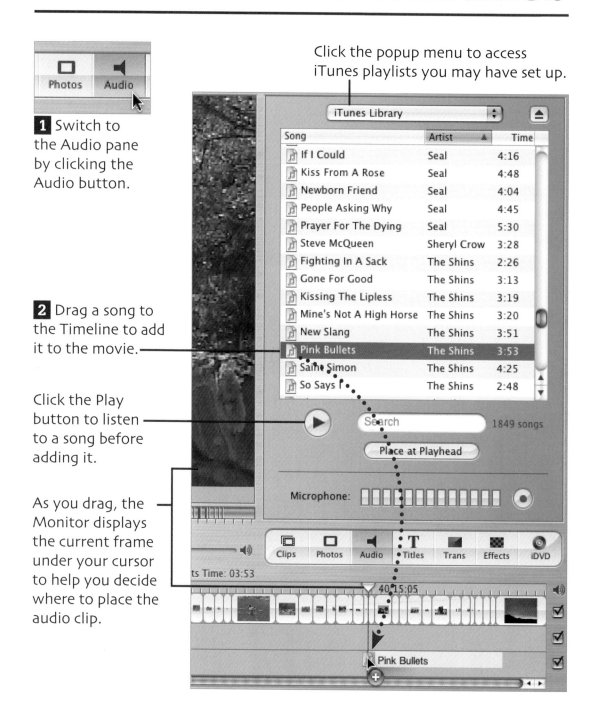

extra bits

import photos p. 26

- Instead of dragging a photo to the Timeline, you can also click the Apply button, which adds the photo to the end of your movie.

- You can add multiple photos at once. Hold down the ⌃⌘ key and click several photos to select them, then drag them to the Timeline.

- In addition to adding pictures stored in iPhoto, you can drag image files from the Finder directly onto iMovie's Shelf or Liquid Timeline.

- If you do drag image files from the Finder, avoid PICT-formatted files—iMovie doesn't display them correctly.

- You can use the Zoom slider to crop still photos, without applying the Ken Burns Effect to them.

- When you import a photo, it's converted to video resolution, and may not look as good onscreen. However, it will look fine when viewed on a television or when exported as a QuickTime file (see Chapter 12).

add motion to photos p. 28

- Click the Reverse button to swap the Start and Finish states (to zoom out instead of zoom in, for example).

- Decide you want to make a change to your Ken Burns Effect settings? Select the clip in the Timeline, change the settings in the Photos pane, and then click the Update button (which normally appears as the Apply button).

- Vertical photos appear in iMovie with black bars to their sides. You could use the Zoom slider to crop the image, but then you're getting only part of the photo. Instead, use the Ken Burns Effect to pan up or down the picture's length.

Original

KBE Start   KBE Finish

extra bits (continued)

add music from iTunes p. 30

- If you know the name of a song or artist that you want to use, type it into the Search field to locate it quickly.

- When you drag a song to your movie, the Timeline Viewer automatically appears to display the audio tracks, even if the Clip Viewer was previously active.

- Unlike video clips, which can be stored on the Shelf, audio clips can only appear on the Timeline. As a temporary holding place, put audio clips at the far right edge of the Timeline.

- Can't see the full name of a song or artist? Click and drag the spaces between the column headers to change the column widths.

- Click the Song, Artist, or Time column header to sort the list. Click it again to reverse-sort the list (such as displaying artists' names that begin with Z at the top). I often click the Time column header to see which songs are short when I know I have only a few seconds of time to fill in my movie.

- It doesn't matter which audio track you place music clips, but I recommend using the lower track; you'll see why in the next chapter.

- GarageBand, which is part of iLife '04, is great for making short segments of background music for your movie. When you export songs from GarageBand, they appear in iTunes—which you can access using the steps outlined in this chapter.

- You can also add music directly from an audio CD. After inserting the CD into your Mac's media drive, switch to the Audio pane, choose the CD from the popup menu, and add songs just as you did from iTunes.

- The Audio pane is also where you can add sound effects. Choose iMovie Sound Effects from the popup menu, then drag an effect to the Timeline.

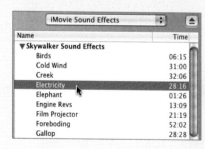

6. edit clips

Now that you've assembled a rough cut of your movie, it's time to start trimming clips and cutting the movie down to make it tight and enjoyable to watch. The editing techniques in this chapter apply to both video and audio clips, including photos (which were rendered as video clips when you added them to the Timeline) and songs you import from iTunes.

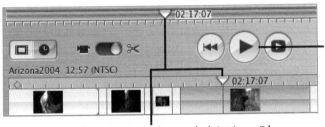

Equally important is seeing how your edits affect clips. The Play button plays your movie in the Monitor starting at the Playhead's location.

However, if a clip is selected, hitting Play shows only that clip in the Monitor.

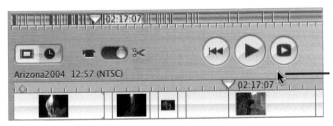

To play the entire movie, deselect the clip by clicking outside the Timeline (such as in the space just above it) and then hit Play.

I want to point out that this chapter differs from the rest in this book because I can't show you how I edit every clip in my movie. Instead, learn about iMovie's different editing techniques from my examples, so that you can apply them to your own footage. View a rough cut of the scene I used while writing this chapter at www.necoffee.com/imovievqs/.

direct-trim clips

iMovie 4 uses an intuitive editing style Apple calls Direct Trimming, which lets you hide the frames you don't want to use.

1 Switch to the Timeline Viewer and select a clip. ——

Timeline Viewer button ——

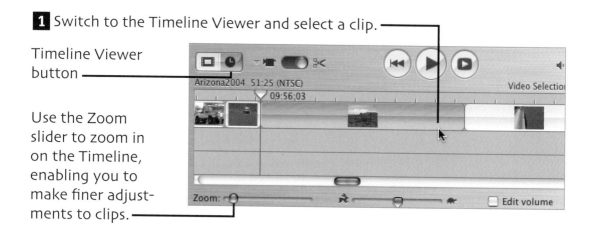

Use the Zoom slider to zoom in on the Timeline, enabling you to make finer adjustments to clips. ——

2 Place the mouse pointer at the edge of the clip. ——

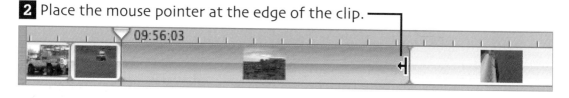

3 Drag to hide frames, then release the mouse button.

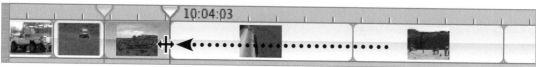

Straight corners indicate direct-trimmed clip. ——

Rounded corners indicate end of clip media.

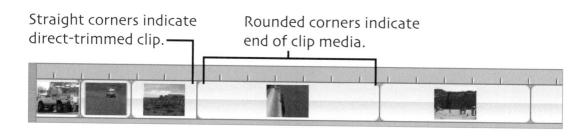

split clips

You can also split clips, just as if you were slicing a strip of film with a razor blade. I often split clips when I know I don't need an entire section, but don't want to click and drag with Direct Trimming.

1 Position the Play-head at the point within a clip where you want to split it.

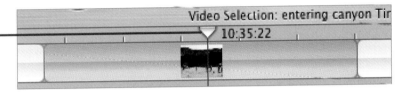

2 Choose Split Video Clip at Playhead from the Edit menu.

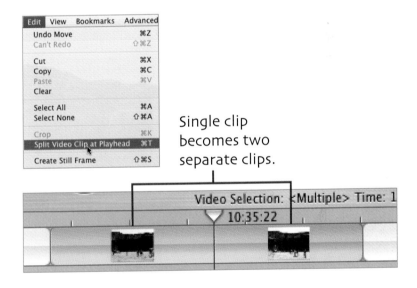

Single clip becomes two separate clips.

First half of original clip deleted.

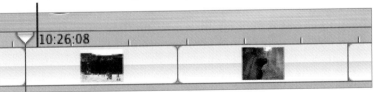

I wanted only the second portion of this clip to appear in my movie, so here I've deleted the first segment. I find that splitting clips and deleting segments (or moving them to the Shelf) is often a faster way of trimming my footage.

crop and trim clips

In addition to editing directly in the Timeline, you can use the Monitor's Scrubber Bar to select a range of frames, then crop or trim the clip. This approach can also be used when editing clips that are still on the Shelf.

1 Select a clip, and position the pointer just below the Scrubber Bar.

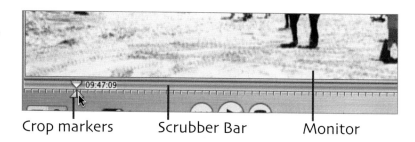

Crop markers   Scrubber Bar   Monitor

2 Drag the crop markers to select a range of frames.

Choose Crop to delete the frames outside the selection.

3 Choose one of the following options from the Edit menu:

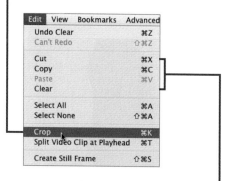

Choose Cut or Clear to delete the frames (trim the clip).

copy and paste

Yes, just like working in a word processor, you can copy and paste frames or entire clips. I use copy and paste when I want to create a new clip out of a selection of frames without breaking up the original clip, in case I want to use the footage somewhere else while I'm editing.

1 Select a range of frames within a clip and choose Copy from the Edit menu.

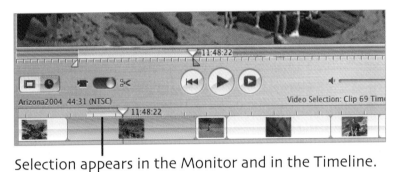

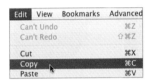

Selection appears in the Monitor and in the Timeline.

2 Select another clip in the Timeline.

3 Choose Paste from the Edit menu.

The copied selection appears as a new clip after the one you had selected.

If no clip is selected before pasting, the new clip appears at the Playhead location, even if that's in the middle of another clip.

Before pasting

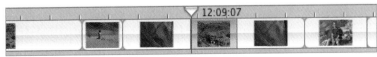

After pasting

paste clips over clips

A common device in movies is to intercut a clip into a scene so that the audio continues to play while the video from a new clip is shown. In iMovie, this is accomplished by pasting a clip over another clip.

1 Open iMovie's preferences and enable this setting (this step is optional, but lets you edit the audio later on).

Other settings: ☑ Extract audio in paste over
☑ Filter audio from camera
☐ Play video through to camera

2 Select a range of frames in a clip you want to use as the flashback and copy them.

3 Position the Playhead where you want the pasted clip to begin.

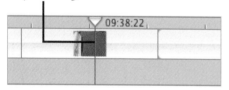

09:38:22

iMovie File **Edit** View Bookmarks Advanced Window Help

Can't Undo	⌘Z
Can't Redo	⇧⌘Z
Cut	⌘X
Copy	⌘C
Paste	⌘V
Clear	
Select All	⌘A
Select None	⇧⌘A
Crop	⌘K
Split Video Clip at Playhead	⌘T
Create Still Frame	⇧⌘S

Movie: Arizona2004 44:08 (NTSC)

4 Choose Paste Over at Playhead from the Advanced menu. The new clip overwrites the existing one...

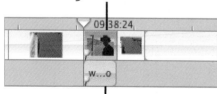

09:38:24

W...O

...but plays the original audio.

Original clip

Pasted clip

Original clip

edit clips

change clip speed

Sometimes, you want to speed up a clip or slow it down. The clip in this example zooms in on a beautiful section of rock, but it goes too fast.

Selected clip, at normal speed

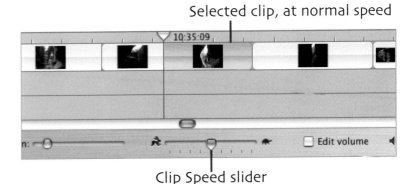

Clip Speed slider

Drag the slider toward the rabbit icon to speed up the clip.

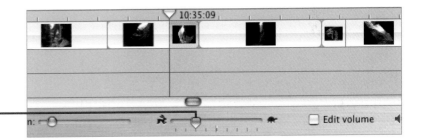

To slow the clip down, drag toward the turtle icon.

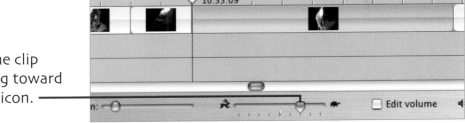

Icons in the Clip Viewer indicate whether a clip has been sped up or slowed down.

Sped-up clip

Slowed-down clip

add color clips

In addition to the footage you imported from your camcorder, and photos you imported from iPhoto, iMovie supports color clips—blank clips that can be used as placeholders or just a solid screen of color.

You may not need to use color clips, but I'm covering them here because you're likely to create one accidentally in the Timeline Viewer: I frequently go to drag the edge of a clip and miss by a few pixels, which ends up dragging the entire clip; you end up with sporadic sections of blank footage in your movie. Here's how to work with (or delete) them.

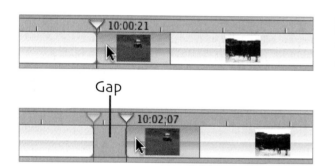

Gap

1 In the Timeline Viewer, drag a clip to the right to expose a gap between clips. During playback, the gap appears as solid black footage.

You can't simply drag the clip back into place, because that creates another gap.

2 Press (Control) and click the gap to bring up the contextual menu, then choose Create Color Clip.

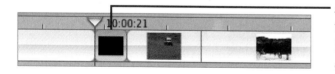

A new color clip is created to fill the gap. If you made the gap by accident, simply delete the color clip to remove the gap.

edit clips

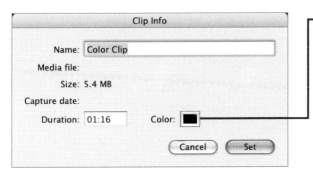

3 To change the color of the clip to something other than black, double-click the clip, which brings up the Clip Info dialog.

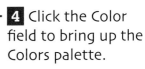

4 Click the Color field to bring up the Colors palette.

5 Drag your pointer in the color wheel to choose a new color.

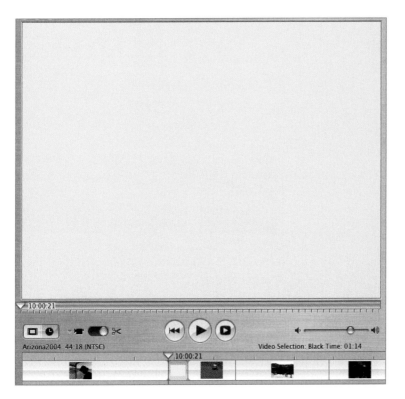

The finished clip can now be used as a colorful transition between scenes, or perhaps as the background of a new title screen (see Chapters 7 and 8 for more information).

restore clips

You've trimmed, split, and cropped a clip to the point where its pieces are strewn all over. Unfortunately, a scene you need is one you had thrown away early in the editing process. At this point it's time to turn to iMovie's tool of last resort: the Restore Clip command.

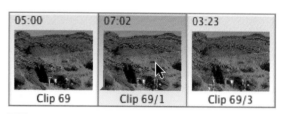

1 Clip 69 has been split into multiple pieces, and Clip 69/2 is missing entirely. Select a clip fragment that you want to restore.

2 Choose Restore Clip from the Advanced menu.

3 iMovie tells you how the clip will be affected. Click OK.

The clip is restored, as you can see by the new duration of 16:23.

change clip volume

Do you have a clip whose volume is too loud or faint? You can change the volume for the entire clip, or for sections within the clip.

In this case, the clip includes loud road noise. One option is to decrease the volume for the entire clip (right), but I'd rather fade the volume down at the beginning, then bring it back up at the end of the clip (below).

Video and audio data are combined in the video clip.

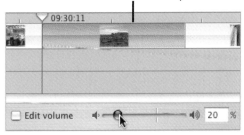

Select a clip, and then drag the Volume slider to change the audio level for the entire clip.

Volume level bar

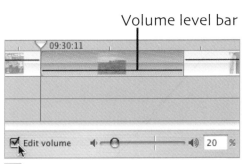

1 To fine tune the volume in a clip, click the Edit volume button.

Beginning point Volume marker

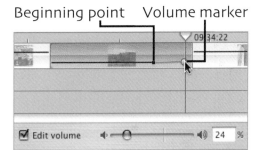

2 Click a point on the volume level bar to set a volume marker.

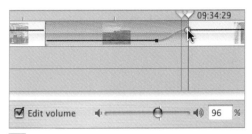

3 Drag the marker to a new level. The curve here indicates a gradual rise in volume.

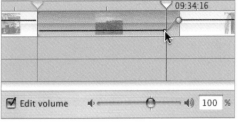

4 Drag the beginning point left or right to set the time it takes for the volume change to occur.

edit clips

extract audio

For more control when editing
audio, extract a clip's audio track.

Extracted audio clip

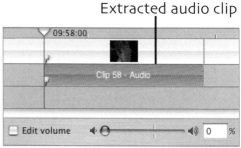

1 Select a video clip.

2 Choose Extract Audio from the
Advanced menu to create a new
clip on the upper audio track.

Audio waveforms

It's easier to edit audio clips when
you can see the audio levels. If
it's not already enabled, turn on
display of waveforms in iMovie's
preferences.

I've also used the Timeline's Zoom
slider to enlarge the appearance
of the audio clip and see more
waveform detail.

lock and unlock audio

Audio lock icons

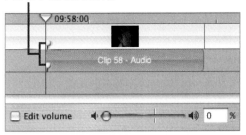

Extracted audio clips are automatically locked to their video clips to keep the audio and video synchronized.

Lock icons removed

To free the extracted audio, click the audio clip and choose Unlock Audio Clip from the Advanced menu.

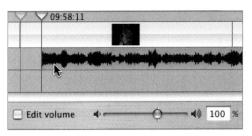

Now you can move the audio clip independently. This is helpful when you want to add the background noise of one video clip to another clip in order to maintain a consistent audio evironment.

When you've repositioned the clip, choose Lock Audio Clip at Playhead from the Advanced menu. As you edit other clips in the movie, the audio remains attached to this new position.

extra bits

direct-trim clips p. 34

- One irritant about clips edited by Direct Trimming is that sometimes you may want some footage that occurs later in the clip. You could split the clip instead (see page 35), but that doesn't help you if you've already used Direct Trimming. Instead, duplicate the clip by choosing Copy and then Paste from the Edit menu. You can then change the trimming on the duplicate clip to display the other scene.

- As you drag the edge of a clip, the Monitor displays the current frame where your cursor is located.

- When dragging a clip's edge, look to the information line above the Timeline to see the clip's new length. If I know I want a clip to last exactly 10 seconds, for example, that's where I look—the timecode near the Playhead indicates the time relative to the entire movie.

Clip length

Video Selection: Clip 51 Time: 10:00 (Monday, 10:54:14

split clips p. 35

- After splitting a clip, each section still contains all of the original footage. Use Direct Trimming to reveal it if you need to.

- If no clip is selected and you choose Split Video Clip at Playhead, only the video clip under the Playhead gets split; audio clips not selected remain intact.

crop and trim clips p. 36

- Initially, the crop markers appear at the far left edge of the Scrubber Bar. You can click and drag anywhere under the bar to activate the crop markers; you don't have to drag them from the left side.

- To deselect frames without applying any edit to them, click another clip or at the top of the Timeline. You can also choose Select None from the Edit menu.

copy and paste p. 37

Consider renaming your newly pasted clip, since it will share the original clip's name.

edit clips

change clip speed p. 39

When you change a clip's playback speed, the audio is also sped up or slowed down. Unless you're going for this effect, set the volume for the clip to zero.

restore clips p. 42

I mentioned this in Chapter 4, but it's worth repeating: don't empty iMovie's Trash! If you do, you will no longer be able to restore your clips; the only way to get them back will be to re-import the footage.

change clip volume p. 43

- To remove a volume marker, click it and then press (Delete).
- You can have as many audio edits as will fit within the clip. This is good for minimizing loud bursts of sound, like someone coughing near the camera.
- When the Edit volume check-box is enabled and you want to select a clip, be sure to click somewhere other than the volume level line to prevent adding an unintentional volume marker.

extract audio p. 44

- Audio waveforms appear only on audio clips, not on video clips. Sometimes it's worth extracting the audio to use the waveforms as guides while editing.
- In addition to using the Zoom slider to zoom in on a clip in the Timeline Viewer, there's another way to see more wave-form detail: with the audio clip selected, press the (↑) or (↓) keys to temporarily enlarge or dimin-ish the waveforms.
- If you later delete an extracted audio clip, the sound isn't gone forever. The original sound is still embedded in the video track, but it's set to zero. Select the clip and increase the volume level. You can then extract the audio again later, if you wish.

edit clips

7. add transitions

As your movie currently stands, each clip is separated by a jump cut, an abrupt switch to the next clip. If you watch movies or television, most shots are separated by jump cuts because they involve no extra work by the editor and because we, as viewers, subconsciously stitch cuts together to form scenes without losing track of what's going on. However, too many jump cuts can be visually jarring, and sometimes it's more appropriate to add some sort of transition that ties two clips together. iMovie includes 13 transitions that will help give your movie a bit more polish.

edit settings

1 Click the Trans button to view the Transitions pane.

2 Position the Play-head near the break between two clips.

3 Click a transition type from the list.

A small preview appears when you click a transition.

4 Change duration using the Speed slider.

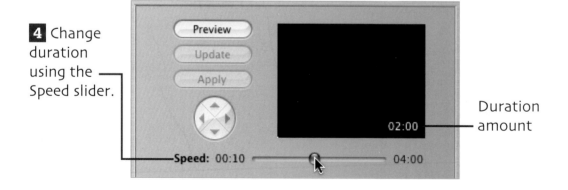

Duration amount

5 If you selected the Push transition, click a direction button to determine from which side the next clip appears.

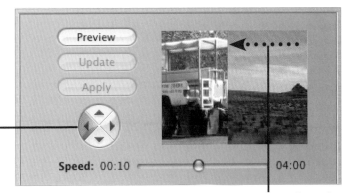

Direction of Push transition

6 For a better idea of how the transition will appear, click the Preview button to play a rough version in the Monitor.

add transitions

add the transition

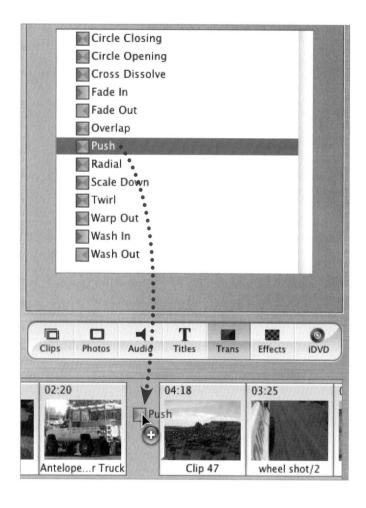

When you've arrived at the settings you want, drag the transition to the Timeline (either the Clip Viewer or Timeline Viewer).

A red bar indicates the rendering progress.

Transition in Clip Viewer

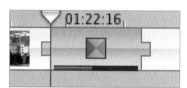

Transition in Timeline Viewer

Is the transition not quite what you expected? You can tweak the behavior at any time by selecting the clip in the Timeline, making adjustments to its settings in the Transitions pane (even changing the type of transition), and then clicking the Update button.

extra bits

edit settings p. 50

- iMovie creates transition previews based on the location of the Playhead. If it's near the beginning of a clip, the transition starts with the previous clip; if it's near the end, the transition starts with the current clip and ends with the next one.

- Several third-party developers have released packages of transitions you can add to iMovie. See Appendix B.

add the transition p. 52

- Unlike regular clips, you can't move transitions. Instead, create a new one for the new location in your movie.

- If you decide you don't want a transition just after you've added it, press ⌘ - . (period) to cancel the rendering process.

- To delete a transition from your movie, simply click it and press Delete.

- During one sequence of my movie, I wanted to use a simple Cross Dissolve transition between several clips. Instead of creating each one individually, select the range of clips (hold ⌘ and click them), choose and configure a transition, and then click the Apply button to add them all at once.

- You can edit volume levels within transitions (see Chapter 6). In fact, some transitions, such as Fade In and Fade Out, automatically adjust the audio levels to fade the sound in or out in tandem with the video.

add transitions

8. add titles

Movie titles weren't always easy to create, which is probably why a movie with a title looks more polished than plain video footage. iMovie gives you several options for adding titles that can appear anywhere within your movie.

create a title

1 Click the Titles button to view the Titles pane.

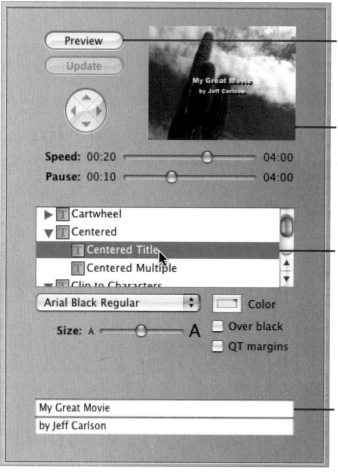

Clicking Preview displays a full-size preview in the Monitor.

A small preview of the title appears over the clip at the current location of the Playhead.

2 Click a title name to select it. Clicking any title displays how the title effect will appear in the small preview window.

3 Type a title into the fields provided. Text in the top field will show up slightly larger than text in the bottom field.

iMovie's titles come in three varieties:

Single shows
two lines of
text at once.

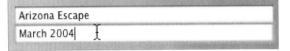

Multiple
shows one
text pair,
then another.

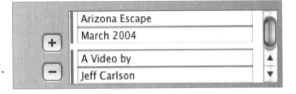

Text block
is used for
longer titles.

Speed
amount

Pause
amount

Total
duration

4 Use the duration
sliders to set the
time that the title
will appear onscreen.

Speed is the time it
takes for the title to
appear; Pause is how
long it stays before
disappearing.

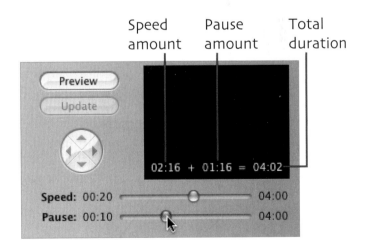

style the text

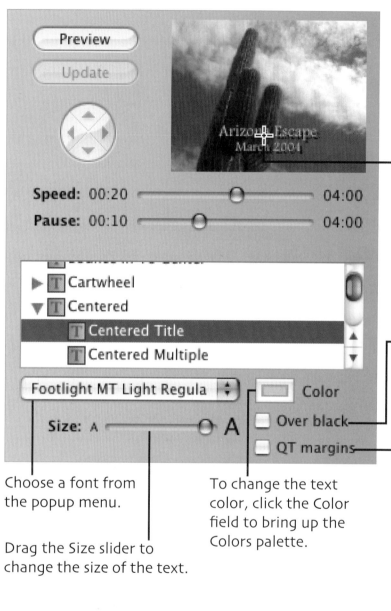

With some titles, you can click the preview window to position the text horizontally. Look for your pointer to change to this icon, then click to position the title.

Click here to create the title on a black background instead of superimposed on a video clip.

To ensure that words don't get cut off when played back on a television, iMovie limits the size of titles. If you know you're going to view your movie only in QuickTime format, click the QT margins box to use the entire frame for titles.

Choose a font from the popup menu.

Drag the Size slider to change the size of the text.

To change the text color, click the Color field to bring up the Colors palette.

add the title

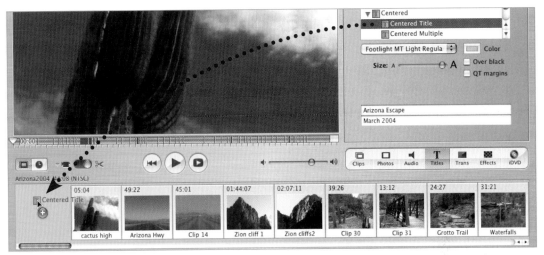

When the title looks as you want it to, drag the title's name from the list to the Timeline (either the Clip Viewer or Timeline Viewer).

Before

This title occupied only part of the clip below it, so a new clip with the remaining footage was created.

After

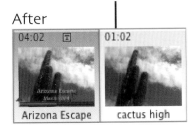

Titles work a bit differently than regular video clips. Think of a title as a clip that's been laid on top of its source clip. Deleting a title restores the original video clip.

If a title is longer than the clip it appears on, the title bleeds over into the next clip and steals some of its footage.

extra bits

create a title p. 56

- iMovie remembers the last text you entered, so if you click another title name, you don't have to re-enter your text.

- When working with titles that feature multiple text pairs, click and drag the pairs to rearrange the order in which they appear.

- Several third-party companies have developed other titles that you can add to iMovie. See Appendix B.

- Some titles include additional controls. For example, Bounce Across features a Wave slider to control how bouncy the text is. Feel free to experiment with the settings.

style the text p. 58

- The size of the title depends on the font you use and the amount of words you type. A title of "Star Wars" will appear larger than "The Empire Strikes Back," even if both are set to the same size.

- With the Colors palette visible, you can click the Preview button to see what the title looks like; you don't need to close the palette.

add the title p. 59

- After adding a title to the Timeline, don't be surprised if the text looks jagged. When viewed on a television, the letters look better.

- You can overlap more than one title if you want. For example, suppose you want a timestamp in the lower-right corner of the screen (using the Music Video title) and a main title in the center (using Centered Title).

- As with transitions (see the last chapter), you can change the settings of an existing title. Click the title in the Timeline, make your adjustments in the Titles pane, and then click the Update button.

- To delete a title, select it in the Timeline and press Delete. The title clip is removed, leaving the original clips it overlapped in the same condition as before the title was applied.

9. add effects

iMovie's effects aren't used as frequently as transitions and titles, mainly because they offer a specific look or action—you just won't have that many occasions to use Fairy Dust. However, some effects are more subtle, such as adjusting a clip's color balance, or applying sepia or black-and-white tone to the footage.

Is it a <u>Star Trek</u> episode, or just iMovie? You can bet I wouldn't put this effect in a vacation movie (but you can view it at www.necoffee.com/imovievqs/).

edit effect settings

1 Click the Effects button to view the Effects pane.

2 Select a clip in the Timeline (using either viewer).

Clicking Preview displays a full-size preview in the Monitor.

The small preview window shows the effect when you click an effect name.

These sliders make the effect appear or disappear gradually (such as blending from Aged Film to normal footage.

3 Click an effect's name to access its controls.

4 Use the sliders to control aspects of each effect.

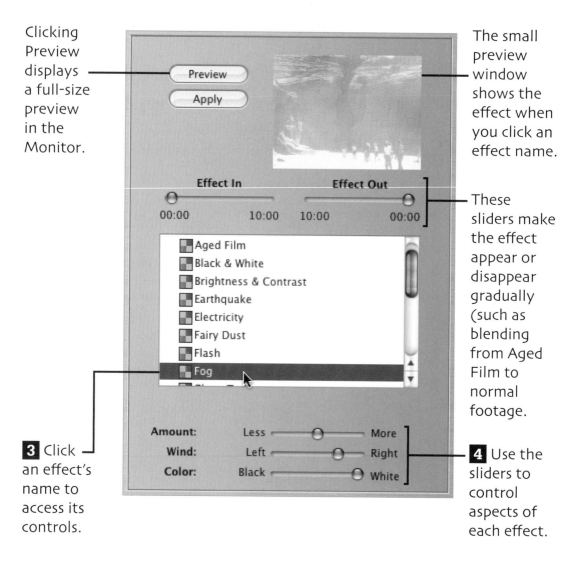

apply the effect

Click Apply to add the effect to your selected clip. Unlike titles and transitions, you cannot drag an effect name to the Timeline.

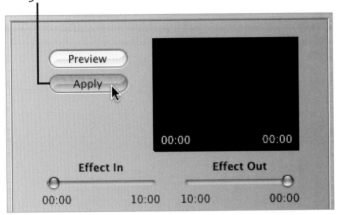

This icon indicates that an effect is applied to the clip.

Multiple effects can be layered upon the same clip, often to surprising results. In this case, I added Soft Focus to Fog and ended up with a spectral look to the clip (hmmm, was it a haunted vacation?).

The number tells you how many effects are applied.

To remove an effect, click the clip to which it's applied and press Delete. The original clip remains intact.

extra bits

edit effect settings p. 62

- If the clip you want to use for an effect has transitions attached to it, applying the effect may remove the transitions (iMovie warns you if this is the case). After adding the effect, simply create the transitions again.

- Some effects, such as Fairy Dust, feature controls in the small preview window. Click within the preview area to determine the angle of the light burst, as in this example (ouch).

apply the effect p. 63

- Unlike titles and transitions, you can't change an effect's settings once the effect has been applied. Instead, you must delete the effect, make your changes, and then re-apply the effect.

- To stop the effect from rendering, press ⌘ - . (period).

- When you delete an effect from a clip that contains multiple effects, you delete only the most–recently-applied effect, not all effects on that clip.

- If you apply some effect types to a still photo, the image needs to be converted to a regular video clip. iMovie warns you if this is about to happen, and gives you the option to cancel.

- Effects cannot be applied to clips on the Shelf. However, you can add an effect to a clip in the Timeline and then move it to the Shelf for later use.

- You can apply transitions and titles to clips that incorporate effects.

add effects

10. share your movie

Before we continue, let's recap our progress so far.

By this point, you've imported your footage from the camera, added any songs and still photos, and assembled the clips in the Timeline. You've also edited the clips and incorporated transitions, titles, and effects.

Before you proceed, make sure any final polishing work has been done on your movie (such as adding other music, trimming clips to tighten the movie's timing, etc.).

In this chapter, you'll share the movie with the rest of the world by emailing it to someone, building a .Mac HomePage (if you're a .Mac subscriber; if not, see the extra bits section on page 71), creating a QuickTime file, and finally creating an iDVD project in preparation for burning the movie to a DVD.

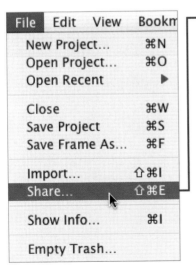

To share a movie, choose Share from the File menu, then follow the instructions in the rest of this chapter.

If you want to share only a section of your movie, select the clips in the Timeline before choosing the Share command.

share via email

1 In the Share dialog, click the Email button.

2 Choose your email program from the popup menu.

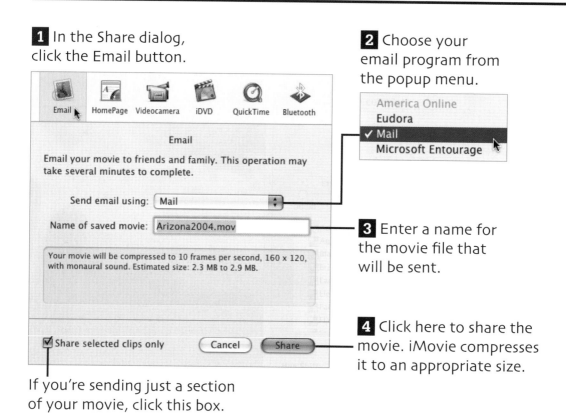

3 Enter a name for the movie file that will be sent.

4 Click here to share the movie. iMovie compresses it to an appropriate size.

If you're sending just a section of your movie, click this box.

5 iMovie launches your email program and creates a new outgoing message with the movie attached (Apple's Mail shown here). Enter a recipient, write a brief note, and hit Send to zing it on its way.

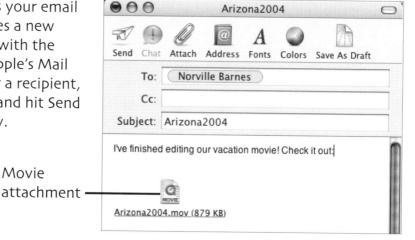

Movie attachment

share your movie

share via a web page

1 In the Share dialog, click the HomePage button.

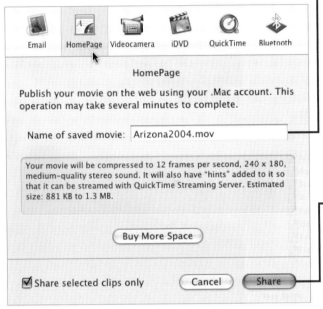

2 Enter a name for the movie file that will appear on the Web.

3 Click Share. iMovie compresses the movie and automatically copies it to your iDisk, then loads the .Mac Web site into your browser. (See extra bits on page 71 if you don't currently have a .Mac account.)

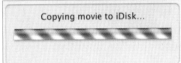

4 After signing into your account, choose a section of your HomePage site, and click an iMovie theme.

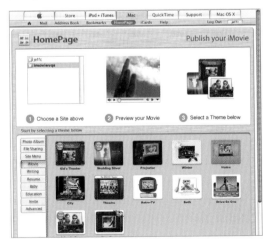

5 Type a page title, movie title, and description into the fields, then click Publish to make the page live.

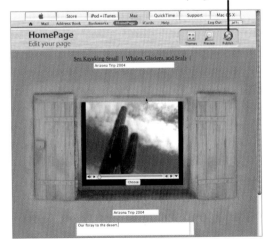

share via QuickTime

1 In the Share dialog, click the QuickTime button.

2 Choose a compression setting from the popup menu (see next page).

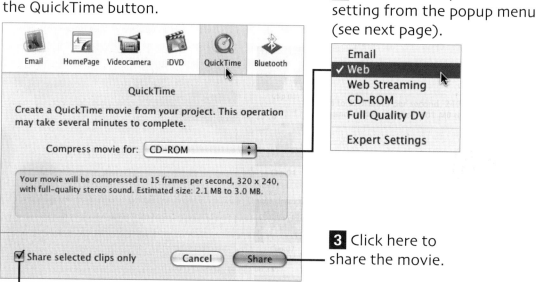

3 Click here to share the movie.

If you're sending just a section of your movie, click this box.

4 In the Save dialog that appears, choose a location on your hard disk.

5 Click Save to compress and save the QuickTime movie file.

You can burn that file to a CD-ROM, upload it to a Web site, or whatever use you see fit for a self-contained movie file.

share your movie

 Email

The preset QuickTime settings are scaled and compressed for their intended medium, so the Email version is smaller in dimension and is more compressed to reduce the file size significantly.

Full Quality DV is not compressed at all, leading to huge file sizes, but the best image quality.

 Web,
Web Streaming

 CD-ROM

 Full Quality DV

create an iDVD project

One advantage of DVDs in general is the ability to jump to specific scenes within a movie, instead of fast-forwarding through the entire movie. You set up these scenes, called chapters, in iMovie before creating the iDVD project.

1 Click the iDVD button.

2 Position the Playhead where you want a chapter to begin.

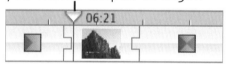

3 Click the Add Chapter button...

...to add a new chapter in the iDVD pane.

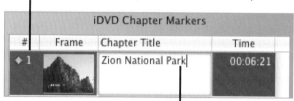

4 Type a name as it will appear in iDVD.

5 After you've added all of your chapters, click the Create iDVD Project button.

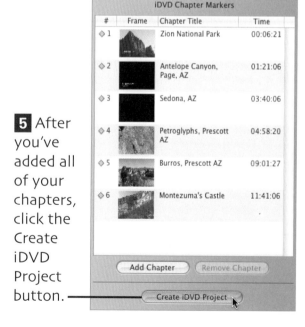

iDVD launches automatically, with your movie already set up in iDVD's main menu screen.

extra bits

share your movie p. 65

- When sharing just a range of clips, the selection must be contiguous—they all need to connect to each other. Otherwise, the "Share selected clips only" option is disabled.

- You can share video clips that are on the Shelf, too. If you select more than one, iMovie assembles them in the order they were originally imported, not their order on the Shelf.

share via email p. 66

- iMovie warns you if the movie's expected file size is too large to send via email. Look in the summary below the file name field.

- Be a responsible Internet citizen: refrain from sending large files (2 MB or larger) via email. A copy of the movie must be stored on every email server between you and your recipient's computer; combined with spam and malicious email attachments floating around out there, this puts a strain on Internet service providers, who may in turn restrict your capability to successfully send large attachments.

share via a web page p. 67

- If you're not a .Mac member, go to www.mac.com to sign up. A one-year membership costs $100, but you can try the service free for 60 days. (Even if you don't choose to pay, you get to keep your .Mac screen name, which is used by iChat AV.)

- At this writing, the .Mac service includes 100 MB of hard disk space. If you find yourself filling that up with movies (or photos or other files), Apple is happy to sell you more space—up to 1 GB of storage (at $350 per year).

- iMovie reads your .Mac membership information when it launches. If you want to publish to another person's account, you need to quit iMovie, make the change in Mac OS X's System Preferences, and then relaunch iMovie.

- You can also publish movies to a .Mac HomePage without doing it directly from iMovie (for example, if you've created a QuickTime movie using custom settings). Copy the movie file to your iDisk, log on to .Mac, click the HomePage icon, and follow the instructions.

extra bits (continued)

share via QuickTime p. 68

- iMovie's default QuickTime settings offer decent image quality and file sizes, but you can do better. Choose Expert Settings from the popup menu, then specify another type of video compression, such as Sorenson Video 3. Apple has more information on its support Web site: http://docs.info.apple.com/article.html?artnum=150115.

- You'll notice that the frame size for Full Quality DV is 720 x 480 pixels, which is a wider screen size than the Monitor's size of 640 x 480. What's going on?

  Although each frame is made up of pixels, the pixels in video are rectangular, not square (taller than they are wide). When viewed in iMovie or iDVD, the size is converted to prevent video from looking squished.

create an iDVD project p. 70

- Clicking a chapter marker in the iDVD pane moves the Playhead to that point in the Timeline.

- You can't move chapter markers. Instead, select a marker in the iDVD pane, click the Remove Chapter button, and then create a new marker in the new location.

- Another method of sharing is to record your movie back to a MiniDV tape in your camcorder, using the Videocamera option in the Share dialog. If you aren't able to burn DVDs, you can connect your camcorder to your television to view the movie.

- If your Mac supports Bluetooth (a short-range wireless network protocol) and you own a Bluetooth-enabled cellular phone, you can share your movie via

11. explore iDVD

Now that you've created an iDVD project (thanks to the tight relationship between iMovie and iDVD), let's look at what you'll be working with.

Arizona2004.dvdproj

Zoo Day.dvdproj

The project file is automatically saved in the Documents folder within your Home directory, with a filename ending in .dvdproj.

iDVD

iMovie

In Chapter 10, iDVD launched when you created the project in the iDVD pane. I should point out that you can also, of course, launch iDVD by double-clicking its application icon or the project file. Like iMovie, iDVD opens the last project that was active.

iDVD's interface

Some themes contain a drop zone, where you can drag photos or movies to customize the menu.

The menu is an editable preview of the first screen of the finished DVD.

The title is the name of the project. A menu can have only one title.

A button is an interactive element on the menu. Each theme draws buttons differently; in this theme, a button is just a text block. When clicked, this button plays the movie from start to finish.

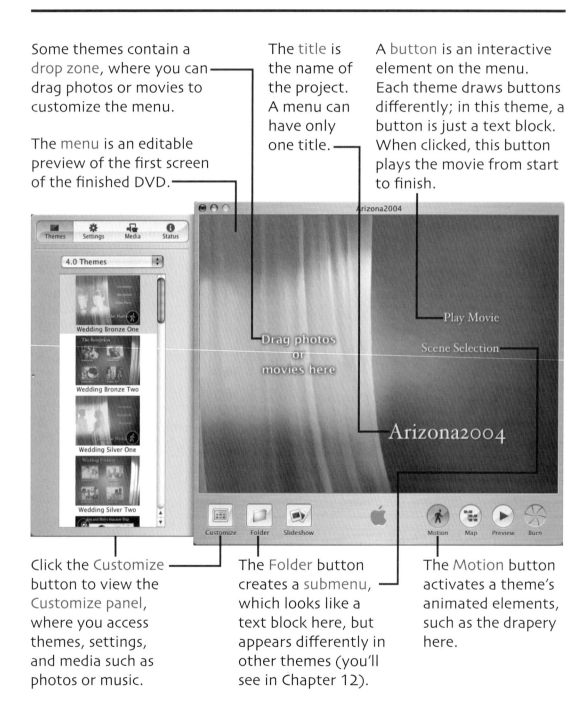

Click the Customize button to view the Customize panel, where you access themes, settings, and media such as photos or music.

The Folder button creates a submenu, which looks like a text block here, but appears differently in other themes (you'll see in Chapter 12).

The Motion button activates a theme's animated elements, such as the drapery here.

Click the Map button to switch to iDVD's Map view (below) which displays your project's structure; click it again to return to the menu. Double-clicking an icon takes you to that menu or movie (except for the AutoPlay well, which works differently; see Chapter 13).

The AutoPlay well lets you play content before the DVD's main menu loads.

Main menu   Button   Submenu

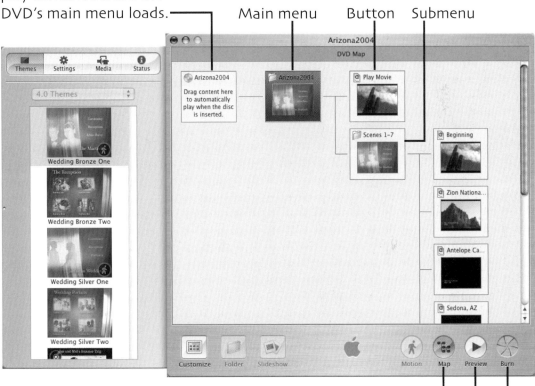

Map button

Click the Preview button (in the Map view or the editing view) to experience the project as if you were viewing it on a DVD player.

When you're ready to create a DVD disc, click the Burn button (asbestos suit not required).

explore iDVD

extra bits

explore iDVD p. 73

- Unlike an iMovie project, which includes subfolders for its media files, an iDVD project contains all the data it needs.
- Closing the iDVD window also quits the program.

iDVD's interface p. 74

- You cannot resize the iDVD window.
- iDVD uses a lot more of your computer's processing power to display motion elements, so unless you're actively working on motion (or you have a wicked-fast Power Mac G5), I recommend turning Motion off while editing your iDVD menus.

12. choose and customize a theme

Instead of starting you off with a blank slate, iDVD offers a selection of professionally designed themes to decorate your DVD menus. You can stick with one of Apple's creations, or customize the look by changing elements of the interface. Either way, you end up with a DVD that looks good, no matter how talented you are in the design department.

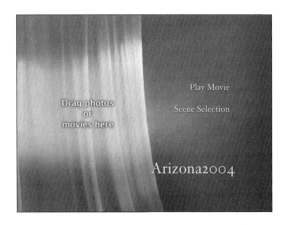

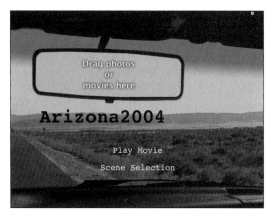

apply a theme

iDVD includes 58 pre-designed themes, ranging from specific topics such as Road Trip to general imagery like Portfolio. I'll choose Road Trip One to match my vacation theme (which even looks a bit like Arizona!).

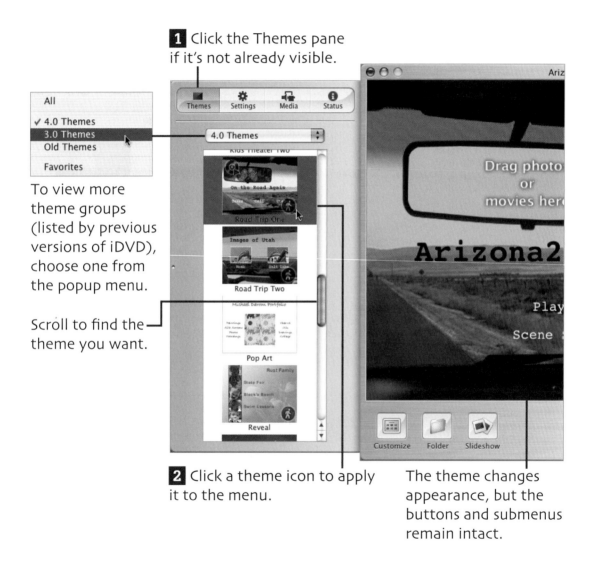

1 Click the Themes pane if it's not already visible.

To view more theme groups (listed by previous versions of iDVD), choose one from the popup menu.

Scroll to find the theme you want.

2 Click a theme icon to apply it to the menu.

The theme changes appearance, but the buttons and submenus remain intact.

choose and customize a theme

edit the title

You can have only one title in a menu, and it behaves a bit differently than other text, depending on the theme. You don't need to select the title to edit its formatting.

1 Click the Settings pane.

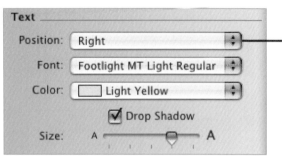

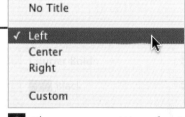

2 Customize the text's appearance by choosing Font, Color, and Size, and whether it should include a drop shadow.

3 Choose a position for the title. The Left, Center, and Right options align the title to a specific area based on the theme. Choose Custom to drag the title anywhere onscreen.

After changing formatting settings

4 If you want to change the title's wording, double-click it to make the text field editable.

5 Type your new title, and then hit (Return) to apply the change.

edit the buttons

Formatting buttons involves two components: the buttons' text (if there is any), and the buttons' shape. When editing buttons, the settings apply to all buttons and submenus on the page. These controls are also found in the Settings pane.

1 Click a button once to select it (if you double-click, it's action will engage, such as playing the movie or opening a submenu).

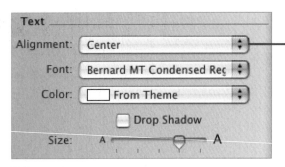

2 Customize the text's appearance by choosing Font, Color, and Size, and whether it should include a drop shadow.

3 Choose an alignment for the button's text. For buttons that are just text, the alignment dictates how the buttons line up in relation to one another.

Aligned left

Aligned right

choose and customize a theme

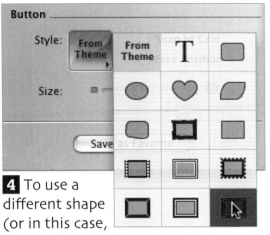

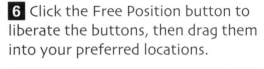

Scene Selection

4 To use a different shape (or in this case, to use a button shape in addition to the text), click the Style popup menu.

The buttons are currently snapped to the underlying grid, which is why they're overlapping.

5 If you want to adjust the button sizes, drag the Size slider.

6 Click the Free Position button to liberate the buttons, then drag them into your preferred locations.

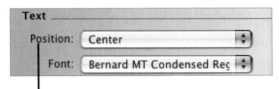

When button shapes are visible, the Alignment popup menu becomes the Position menu, which controls the position of text relative to the button.

choose and customize a theme

edit motion buttons

Buttons don't have to be static pictures. Part of iDVD's Motion features are motion buttons. A button that leads to a movie can play a portion of the movie in the button's thumbnail image. If the button leads to a submenu containing movie clips, you can choose which clip's starting frame appears in place of the generic folder icon.

If you don't want the movie to play in the button's shape, deselect this checkbox. You can still choose a starting frame to use as an icon.

  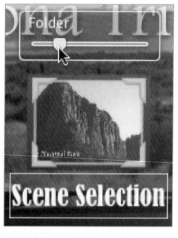

1 Click a button once to select it.

2 Drag the Movie slider to locate the frame you wish to use as the starting point.

Submenu buttons work the same way: drag the Folder slider to locate an image to use as the button's icon.

3 To see how the buttons play back, click the Motion button. Click it again to turn motion off.

choose and customize a theme

add drop zone video

Several iDVD themes include a drop zone, an area that can accept video or image files to add more visual interest. In this case, I'm going to see how the menu looks when I add a video.

1 Click the Media pane.

2 Choose Movies from the popup menu.

3 Drag a movie file from the list to the drop zone. In this example, I exported a section of my movie to a QuickTime file (see Chapter 10).

When Motion is enabled, the movie plays back in the drop zone.

The media disappears in a puff of smoke.

To remove drop zone video or photos, click and drag the contents out of the zone.

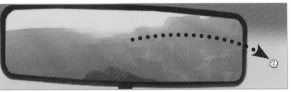

add drop zone photos

In addition to video, you can add photos from iPhoto. Using one photo makes for a pretty picture, but adding several creates a slideshow in the drop zone area.

1 Choose Photos from the popup menu.

2 Select one or more photos from the list.

iDVD tells you how many pictures are being added.

3 Drag the selected photos to the drop zone to add them.

         choose and customize a theme

4 Click the drop zone, and use the Photos slider to choose which photo appears first in the slideshow.

5 Click and drag within the drop zone to reposition the photo. Be careful not to drag outside the zone.

6 Would you like to rearrange the order in which the photos appear? Click the Edit Order button to bring up the Drop Zone Editor.

To delete a photo, select it and press (Delete).

7 Drag the thumbnails to change the order.

You can also drag more photos (up to 30) from the Media pane to the Drop Zone Editor to add them to the slide-show.

8 When you're finished, press the Return button in the lower-right corner of the Drop Zone Editor to go back to the menu.

change background

A dramatic way to customize your menu is to replace a theme's background image with one of your own, either a photo or a movie.

Drag a photo from the Media pane to the menu's background.

Changing the background with this technique retains the drop zone, which may not be ideal in your design (but may work with other themes).

Another method is to drag a media file to the Settings tab...

...and, after the Settings pane appears (without releasing the mouse button), drag the file to the Background well.

With this approach, however, the drop zone is hidden by the background image.

choose and customize a theme

set background audio

DVD isn't just a visual medium—
you can add your own music
that will play while the menu is
onscreen. Some themes already
include background music.

1 In the
Media pane,
choose Audio
from the pop-
up menu.

2 Locate the song
you want to use.

3 Drag the song to the menu's background.
It will play while Motion is enabled.

As with drop zones, you can remove a song by dragging
it out of the Audio well, where it disappears in a puff of
smoke. (The same applies to removing background images
out of the Background well.)

apply submenu theme

Your main menu is now done, so it's time to turn to the submenu that iDVD automatically created to access the chapters you set up in iMovie.

1 Double-click the icon for the submenu to load it into the editing screen.

Buttons access the movie chapters.

iDVD assigns a default theme to the submenu.

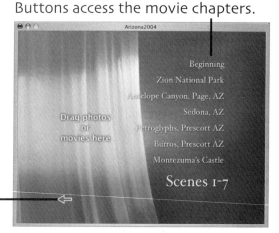

Navigation arrow takes you to the main menu.

2 Choose a new theme in the Themes pane.

3 Using the steps you learned throughout this chapter, customize the look of the buttons and other elements of the submenu.

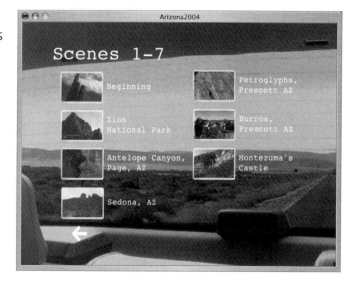

choose and customize a theme

extra bits

apply a theme p. 78

- If 58 built-in themes aren't enough for you, consider buying themes from other developers. See Appendix B.
- Some themes include background music when the Motion button is enabled. That's fine for playing the DVD on a television, but can be grating while editing. I usually activate Motion only when I need to view animated elements.

edit the title p. 79

When using the Custom position for the title, remember that most television screens cut off part of the visible image. Choose Show TV Safe Area from the Advanced menu to view recommended boundaries.

edit the buttons p. 80

To make multiple-line button titles, simply hit Return between words.

edit motion buttons p. 82

Is nothing happening when you click the Motion button? Go to the Settings pane, and check the Duration slider—it may have gotten set to zero. Duration controls how much of the menu's motion plays before starting over. Typically, this amount is the menu's longest background movie or audio, but you can set it lower.

add drop zone video p. 83

- If you'd rather not see the drop zone text ("Drag photos…"), go to iDVD's preferences and uncheck Show Drop Zones. The zones are still there, just not explicitly marked.
- You can also drag video files from the Finder to a drop zone, instead of using the Media pane.
- A drop zone video plays back from the beginning of the clip; you can't choose a starting frame the way you can with motion buttons.

extra bits (continued)

add drop zone photos p. 84

- The length of time each photo appears onscreen depends on how many photos you've added, and the Duration amount. The fewer the photos, the longer each will be visible.

- You can drag image files from the Finder to drop zones, too.

- It's not possible to resize or crop drop zone photos within iDVD.

- If you've already added photos to a drop zone, dragging more to the zone replaces the ones you have. Use the Drop Zone Editor instead.

- In the Drop Zone Editor, you can view the photos in a list by clicking the view preference buttons in the upper-right corner of the screen.

change background p. 86

- If you want to use a movie as a background image (also known as a motion menu), you need to drop it on the Background well—otherwise, the movie becomes a button. Also, export it from iMovie as a Full Quality DV QuickTime movie to get the best image quality.

- If you switch to a new theme, your custom background is deleted; you'll have to add it again to the new theme.

set background audio p. 87

- You can drag a QuickTime movie to the Audio well, which will use only its audio track.

- The music loops created in GarageBand make for great background music on a DVD.

- When you drag a song onto the Audio well in a theme that already has background music, your song takes precedence. If you remove your song from the well, the theme's song is still there—you need to delete that, too, if you want no background audio.

apply submenu theme p. 88

For a little more visual snazz, apply a transition between menus. Choose one from the Transition menu in the Settings pane. Also note that transitions play only when going to a submenu, not when returning to the previous menu.

13. add more content to the DVD

The iDVD project has been pretty straightforward so far: you've added chapters to an edited iMovie video, tossed it into iDVD, and edited the project's theme to make it look slick and polished. In this chapter, you'll add a few more things to the project: an additional submenu, other movies, a photo slideshow, and DVD-ROM data that is stored on the disc and accessible to people using computers instead of commercial DVD players.

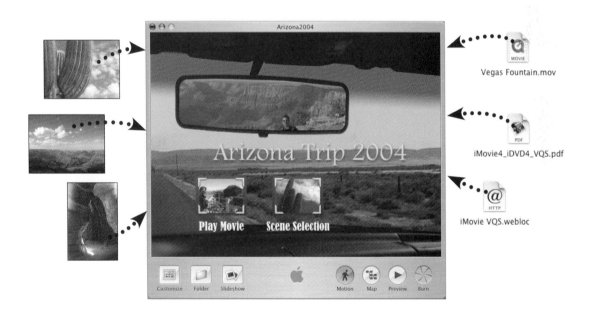

create a submenu

You already have one submenu in your project—the Scene Selection folder that contains each chapter of your movie. However, since you'll be adding more content in this chapter, let's create a new submenu to store it.

 1 Click the Folder icon to create a new submenu.

 **2** Enter a custom title (instead of "My Folder"), and double-click its icon to open it.

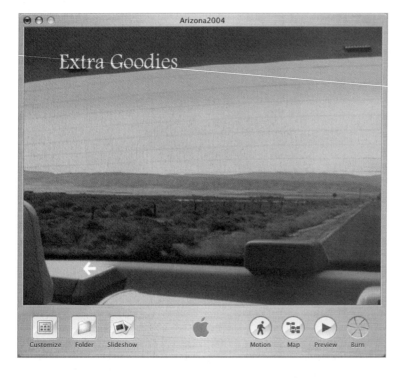

3 Apply a theme and edit the text as you did in the last chapter.

Here's a simplified map showing where the submenu fits in:

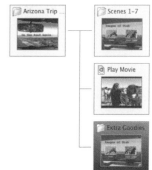

add movies

I wanted to share a clip that didn't make it into my final edited movie. I used iMovie's Share feature to save it as a QuickTime file (see Chapter 10), which I can now bring into iDVD.

1 Click the Media pane.

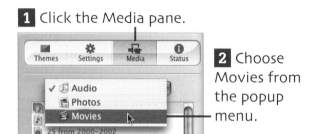

2 Choose Movies from the popup menu.

3 Drag a movie clip to the menu.

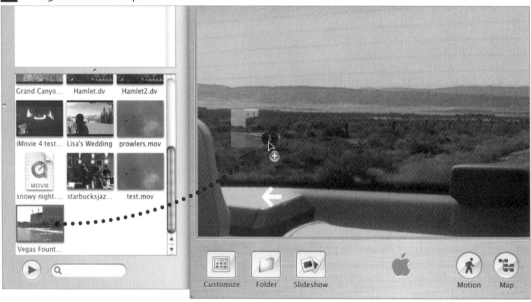

The movie appears as a new button, which you can edit as described in the last chapter.

create a slideshow

In Chapter 5, you added photos to your iMovie project. Once incorporated into your movie, however, the photos get converted to video clips. In iDVD, you can build a slideshow that presents your photos sequentially, with transitions between each one and a soundtrack in the background. Although you could accomplish something similar in iMovie, it's much easier to do it here.

1 Choose Photos from the popup menu.

2 Drag an album to the menu.

In iPhoto, I made an album of my favorite photos. It's easier to drag an album into iDVD, but you can also select the photos you want and drag them in as a group to create a new slideshow.

If you make a habit of naming your pictures in iPhoto, type a photo's title in the Search field to find it quickly.

You can also click the Slideshow button to create an empty slideshow, but dragging an album or photos is much easier.

3 Click the slide-show's button and use the slider to select a photo to use as an icon.

4 Double-click the new slideshow to access the Slideshow editor.

5 Set options for the slideshow.

Drag photos to rearrange them, or select them and press [Delete] to clear them.

Click to replay the slideshow from the beginning.

Click to show navigation arrows on photos.

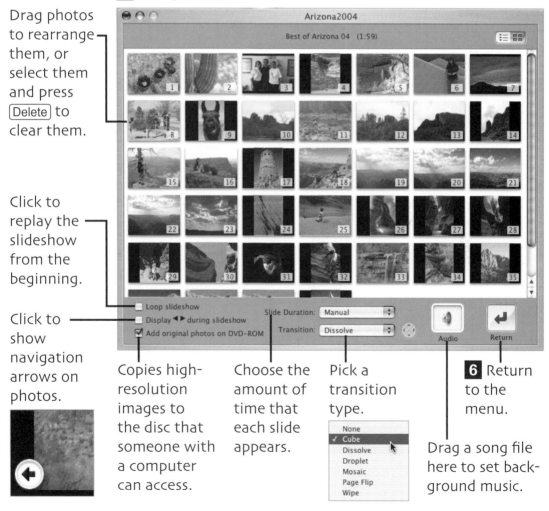

Copies high-resolution images to the disc that someone with a computer can access.

Choose the amount of time that each slide appears.

Pick a transition type.

6 Return to the menu.

Drag a song file here to set back-ground music.

add DVD-ROM content

The acronym DVD stands for "digital versatile disc" because you can store more than just movies on the shiny silver platters. iDVD can create a DVD-ROM (read-only media) area of a disc containing files that are accessible when the disc is inserted into a Mac or PC with a DVD drive.

1 iDVD manages DVD-ROM content separate from its theme-driven interface. Choose Edit DVD-ROM Contents to begin.

2 Drag files from the Finder to the DVD-ROM Contents window to add them.

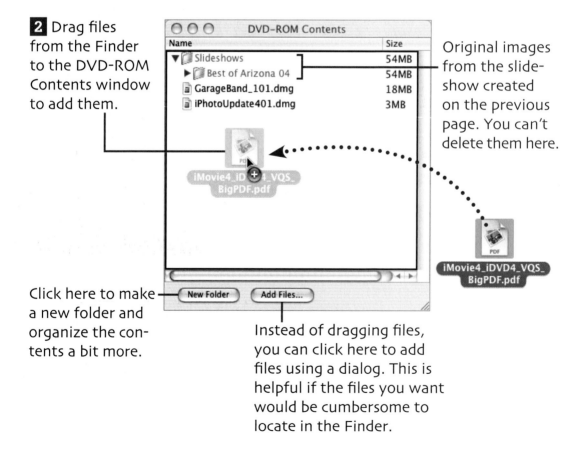

Original images from the slide-show created on the previous page. You can't delete them here.

Click here to make a new folder and organize the contents a bit more.

Instead of dragging files, you can click here to add files using a dialog. This is helpful if the files you want would be cumbersome to locate in the Finder.

extra bits

create a submenu p. 92

Submenus are often created when you've run out of room for all the buttons on one menu. If you're facing button overload, there's an easy way to move some of those items to a new submenu: select them, and choose New Menu from Selection from the Project menu. However, you can't go back and move them to the previous menu, except through the Undo command.

add movies p. 93

- When you drag a movie file from the Finder to your menu, make sure you don't release it over a drop zone.

- Closing the iDVD window also quits the program.

- For the best quality, try to use QuickTime files that were saved as Full Quality DV (if they came from iMovie).

- Many DVDs these days include a short bit of video that plays before the menu loads. To do this, click the Map button and drag a movie file to the Auto-Play well in the upper-left corner of the map.

create a slideshow p. 94

- Click the Preview button while in the Slideshow editor to watch your slides without previewing the full DVD menu.

- To make photos appear better in iDVD, crop them first in iPhoto using the 4 x 3 (DVD) option under the Constrain popup menu.

- You can create slideshows by dragging photos from the Finder or even directly from iPhoto's main window.

- Consider dragging a bunch of photos to the AutoPlay well in the Map view to start your DVD with a slideshow before the menu loads.

- When picking an image to use as the slideshow button's icon, use the ⬅ or ➡ keys to view the photo thumbnails instead of dragging the slider.

- iDVD automatically scales slideshow photos to fit within the TV Safe Area. To use the full screen, open iDVD's preferences, click the Slideshow icon, and disable the option labeled "Always scale slides to TV Safe area".

extra bits (continued)

add DVD-ROM
content p. 96

- DVD-ROM content can be nearly any file on your Mac. For example, you could include Web links (such as those created when you drag a URL out of Safari to the Desktop), PDFs containing more information about your vacation destination, maps, etc.

- Feel free to rearrange the items in the DVD-ROM Contents window by dragging them into whatever order you like.

- When you set up DVD-ROM content, iDVD only creates a link to the files you've specified; the original files aren't copied until you burn the disc. If you delete or move a file to a new location in the Finder, you'll get a "File not found" message. Either move the file to its previous location, or delete the reference in the DVD-ROM Contents window and add the file again.

add more content to the DVD

14. burn the DVD

In Hollywood, shooting and editing a film is only the first half of the process. No matter how good the movie may be, without distribution it's going to sit anonymous on a shelf.

You're probably not aiming for a screening at the Sundance Film Festival, but currently your movie exists only on your hard disk. Now is the time to put that iDVD editing to work and burn your project to disc.

Before jumping in, I need to cover a few DVD basics you need to know in advance.

Although several flavors of blank DVDs are on the market, the only type that works with iDVD is DVD-R (not to be confused with DVD+R, DVD+RW, or DVD-RW).

DVD-R discs come in 1x, 2x, 4x, and 8x speeds. This is a measurement of how fast the SuperDrive's laser can carve data into a disc's surface.

Check the specifications of your Mac at Apple's support site to see at what speed your SuperDrive operates: www.info.apple.com/support/applespec.html.

Also, before you burn any DVD disc, make sure your SuperDrive's firmware has been updated—on some models, using 4x-speed DVD-R media can damage the drive! Read more about it at docs.info.apple.com/article.html?artnum=86130.

(You can find the URLs above, along with other related information, at this book's companion Web site: www.necoffee.com/imovievqs/.)

Lastly, remember that a DVD-R disc can store roughly 4.7 GB of data (compared to CD-Rs, which hold about 700 MB). That means you'll need to have plenty of free hard disk space available when it comes time to encode (prepare) the data and burn it to the disc.

preview the DVD

Use iDVD's Preview mode to see how the DVD
will operate when played back on a DVD player.

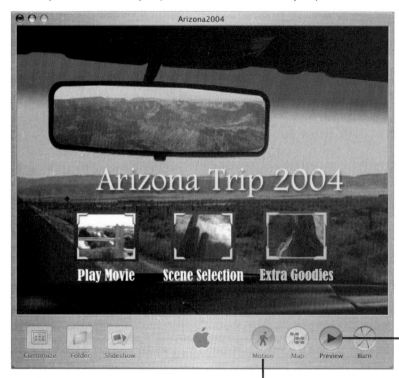

A virtual remote
control device
appears so you
can test how the
menu items will
work.

Click the Preview
button to enter
Preview mode.

Enable Motion to see animated elements in the preview.

A slideshow
or video
footage
plays back
in iDVD's
window.

burn the DVD

set encoding options

Before a project is burned to disc, iDVD encodes the data into a format that DVD players will recognize. This process also compresses your movie's gigabytes of video footage into a size that will fit on the disc. iDVD offers two types of encoding options, which you access from iDVD's preferences.

The default setting is Best Performance, which offers the fastest encoding time. However, your movie must be less than 60 minutes, including other assets such as motion elements.

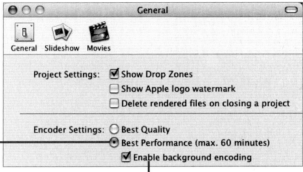

For projects of up to 2 hours in length, choose Best Quality. At burn time, iDVD analyzes the movie to determine the best level of compression while retaining image and sound quality.

An advantage of Best Performance is that iDVD can encode the data in the background while you work, shortening the overall burn time.

This means Best Quality offers no background encoding, but you gain an extra 60 minutes' worth of footage on disc.

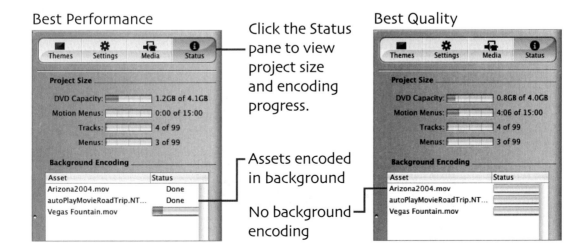

Best Performance

Click the Status pane to view project size and encoding progress.

Best Quality

Assets encoded in background

No background encoding

burn the DVD

1 Finally, time to burn! Click the Burn button once to activate it.

3 When prompted, insert a blank DVD-R disc in your Mac's SuperDrive.

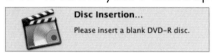

Disc Insertion...
Please insert a blank DVD-R disc.

2 Click the button again to start the disc burning process.

4 Wait. Get some coffee. Go to bed. Depending on your project's size, iDVD can take hours to encode and burn the disc. After Stage 4, below, the disc ejects and you're done!

Stage 1. iDVD checks that it has the pieces it needs to continue the burning process.

Stage 1: Preparing...

Cancel

Stage 2. Buttons, motion menus, and other interface elements are rendered and encoded. Slideshow transitions get processed here, too.

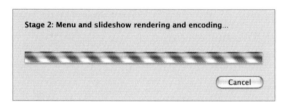

Stage 2: Menu and slideshow rendering and encoding...

Cancel

Stage 3. The heavy lifting—if you're using Best Quality, the entire movie is scanned to determine the best compression quality, then the footage is rendered.

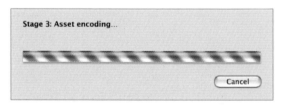

Stage 3: Asset encoding...

Cancel

Stage 4. "Multiplexing" combines the audio and video data into a single stream that DVD players can read. Burning is when the laser etches data into the disc's surface.

Stage 4: Multiplexing and burning...

Cancel

create project archive

What's that you say? You don't currently own a Mac with a SuperDrive? Not a problem! You can save an iDVD project as an archive, then take that archive to someone else who owns a SuperDrive. An archive is also good if you want to build a project on one computer, but do the encoding and burning on a faster Mac.

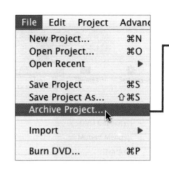

1 Choose Archive Project from the File menu.

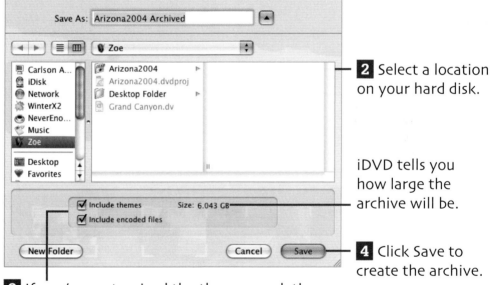

2 Select a location on your hard disk.

iDVD tells you how large the archive will be.

4 Click Save to create the archive.

3 If you've customized the theme, mark the Included themes checkbox to ensure that all of the data will be present on the destination Mac.

Select Include encoded files if you want to save the encoding that's been done already, even though it will make the archive file size larger.

extra bits

preview the DVD p. 100

- When you exit the preview during a slideshow, you're taken directly to the Slideshow editor instead of the menu.
- Clicking Exit on the remote control takes you out of Preview mode.

set encoding options p. 101

- Remember that Best Quality does not encode in the background. Many people mistakenly wait for the progress bars in the Status pane to appear, to no avail. Encoding begins when you burn the disc.
- If you're using Best Performance with Background Encoding turned on, wait until the assets have finished encoding before you burn the disc.
- Projects longer than 60 minutes are more likely to have reduced image quality due to the higher degree of compression required to fit on a disc.
- Use the DVD Capacity figure to gauge how much space your project will occupy on the disc. Also, the numbers change depending on whether Motion is enabled or not.

burn the dvd p. 102

- Make sure you have plenty of hard disk space before you burn: at least twice the size of your project.
- Enable the Motion button before burning to make sure motion elements are included.
- Blank CDs can be bought for pennies apiece, but DVDs are still on the higher edge of the price range. However, buying in bulk from online stores such as www.shop4tech.com, or www.dealnews.com can get you prices below $1 per disc.
- Remember that the total space occupied on the disc includes motion menus, slideshows, and the like. So, if your movie is 52 minutes long, you may still get an error message that the project is too big.
- Including transitions between menus or within slideshows increases the burning time.
- After your DVD is burned, label it with a permanent marker; adhesive labels can unbalance the disc during play and potentially damage your DVD player.
- Test the DVD on several DVD players and computers.

appendix a:
troubleshooting

No one wants to run into trouble, but unfortunately it does happen. The suggestions in this appendix can help if iMovie or iDVD is crashing, or if the program's performance is choppy.

For more specific queries, turn to the Web and the large community of iMovie and iDVD users who share their experiences. The first place I look is Dan Slagel's "Unofficial" iMovie FAQ (frequently asked questions). Apple's discussion forums are also filled with information. See Appendix B for those URLs, or go to my own iMovie/iDVD Web site at www.necoffee.com/imovievqs/.

Also, make sure you're running the latest versions of iMovie, iDVD, and QuickTime (especially the latter). Apple's iLife Web page (www.apple.com/ilife/) includes links to the latest updates. To check your versions, go to the iMovie or iDVD menu in each program, and choose About iMovie or About iDVD.

For QuickTime, go to Software Preferences, click the QuickTime icon, and click the About QuickTime button.

Software version numbers

improve performance

Make the iMovie window smaller. Drag the resize handle in the lower-right corner of the screen to make the window smaller.

Quit other running applications. iMovie and iDVD will gladly use as much memory and processor power as you can throw at them. If playback is sluggish, try running only iMovie or iDVD.

Delete the program's preferences. If iMovie or iDVD crashes, its preferences can become corrupted, causing more problems later. Here's how to delete preferences:

1 Quit the application.

2 In the Finder, choose Home from the Go menu.

3 Open the Library folder.

4 Open the Preferences folder.

5 Delete the following files (you may not have them all):

> iMovie Preferences
> com.apple.imovie.plist
> com.apple.iMovie3.plist
> com.apple.iDVD.plist

Turn off FileVault (Mac OS X 10.3). FileVault is a technology introduced in Mac OS X 10.3 Panther that creates an encrypted version of your Home directory to secure its contents from snooping eyes. The problem is that iMovie and iDVD store their project files in the Home directory by default. So, when FileVault is active, the computer is constantly encrypting and decrypting massive quantities of data on the fly. Turn FileVault off in Mac OS X's Security preference pane.

Make sure you have plenty of available hard disk space. I can't say it enough. Digital video requires huge amounts of disk space. Consider buying an external hard drive and storing your projects there; if your Mac includes a FireWire 800 port (a faster version of FireWire), get a drive with FireWire 800 support.

troubleshoot burning

Check your DVD media. Sometimes a failed burn operation is the fault of the disc. This can happen with generic discs bought in bulk, but also occurs with more reputable vendors' discs. Try a new brand of disc, starting with the ones Apple sells (since presumably they've been vetted by the company).

Also, make sure you're using DVD-R discs, not DVD-RW, DVD+R, or DVD+RW.

Clean your SuperDrive. Accumulated dust can disrupt the laser used to burn data to a disc. Spray a little compressed air into the SuperDrive's slot to blow the dust away.

Set Energy Saver settings. Since it can take hours to burn a disc, your computer may think you've left it and go into a power-saving mode. In Mac OS X's System Preferences, set the processor performance to Highest and the hard drive to never spin down. Also turn off the option to put the computer to sleep automatically after a period of inactivity.

Burn during the day. Many people do their disc burning at night while they sleep (computers are meant to do work while we rest, aren't they?). If you're waking up to burn failures, try burning during the day—Mac OS X performs some nightly maintenance operations around 3 a.m., which could be interfering with the burning operation.

Change audio quality. iMovie and iDVD use audio set to 48.000 kHz (16-bit). However, some audio sources may record at 44.100 kHz, which has been known to cause burning problems. Take these steps to change a movie's audio quality:

1 Export your movie from iMovie to a QuickTime file using Expert Settings.

2 In the Movie Settings dialog, under Sound options, click the Settings button.

3 Click the Rate popup menu and choose 48.000.

4 Export the clip, then import it into iDVD.

troubleshoot system

Repair Mac OS X permissions. When things start going haywire under Mac OS X, I take this step first. Each file on your computer has permissions assigned to it, which dictate, for example, how the file can be changed or moved. For whatever reason, sometimes the wrong permissions get applied.

1 Open Disk Utility, which is located in the Utilities folder within your Applications folder.

2 Choose your startup disk.

3 Click to repair permissions.

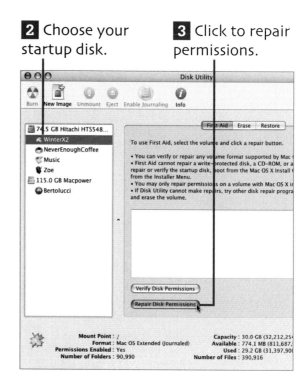

appendix b:
resources

Making a Movie in iMovie & iDVD: Visual QuickProject Guide, companion Web site

http://www.necoffee.com/imovievqs/

Apple iLife

http://www.apple.com/ilife/

Apple's iMovie Support

http://www.apple.com/support/imovie/

Apple's iMovie Discussion Forums

http://discussions.info.apple.com/iMovie/

Apple's iDVD Support

http://www.apple.com/support/idvd/

Apple's iDVD Discussion Forums

http://discussions.info.apple.com/idvd/

reference and tutorials

The "Unofficial" iMovie FAQ

http://www.danslagle.com/mac/iMovie/

Ken Tidwell's "Unofficial" iDVD FAQ

http://www.kentidwell.com/idvd4/

MacDV Mailing List

http://lists.themacintoshguy.com/Lists/MacDV/List.html

iMovieFest

http://www.imoviefest.com/

Cyber Film School

http://www.cyberfilmschool.com/

DVcreators.net

http://www.dvcreators.net/

2-pop.com

http://www.2-pop.com/

Post Forum

http://www.postforum.com/

iMovie software

GeeThree

http://www.geethree.com/

Granted Software

http://www.grantedsw.com/still-life/

eZedia

http://www.ezedia.com/

Virtix

http://www.virtix.com/

Stupendous Software

http://www.stupendous-software.com/

cf/x

http://www.imovieplugins.com/

BKMS

http://plugins.bkms.com/

Freeplay Music

http://www.freeplaymusic.com/

Killer Sound, Inc.

http://www.killersound.com/

Sound Dogs

http://www.sounddogs.com/

iDVD software

iDVD ThemePak

http://www.idvdthemepak.com/

Blue Fusion iDVD Themetastic

http://www.idvd-themetastic.com/

glossary

Burn. The (rather lengthy) process of etching data into a DVD disc's surface to create a disc that a consumer DVD player or computer with a DVD drive can read.

Clip. A segment of video or audio.

Clip fragment. Remnant of an audio or video segment, sometimes caused by overzealous cropping or trimming.

Clip Speed slider. This control lets you adjust the speed of your footage, clip by clip. You'll recognize the Clip Speed slider by its rabbit and turtle icons, just below the Liquid Timeline.

Clip Viewer. One of two modes of the Liquid Timeline, the Clip Viewer displays clips in play order, using large thumbnail previews to help you identify them.

Clip Viewer button. Filmstrip icon that appears above the Liquid Timeline. Click this icon to display the Clip Viewer.

Clips pane. This virtual display case, also known as the Shelf, sits to the right of the Monitor. Your video clips are stored here, arranged on a grid. Use the scroll bar to view more clips.

Color clips. Whether black, cobalt, or any other available hue, color clips are placeholders added between video clips.

Insert these clips to help you adjust and perfect the timing of your movie.

Crop. Delete frames that are outside a selected portion of a clip. Choose Crop from the Edit menu.

Crop markers. These triangular shapes appear when you position the mouse pointer just below the Scrubber Bar. Click and drag these markers to select a portion of your clip.

Cross Dissolve. Commonly used transition where the end of one clip fades into the beginning of the next clip.

Customize panel. The area where most of iDVD's options and controls are stored. It houses the Themes, Settings, Media, and Status panes.

Direct Trimming. A click-and-drag editing technique, performed in the Timeline Viewer. Shortening clips by Direct Trimming works faster than cropping, and allows unwanted frames to be hidden instead of deleted. Clips with a straight edge (or two) have been trimmed.

Drop zone. A special area in several iDVD themes where photos or movies can play within the menu to add more visual interest.

glossary

DVD. Short for Digital Versatile Disc, this plastic platter packs nearly seven times the data into the same space as a compact disc: a CD stores roughly 700 MB, while a DVD holds approximately 4.7 GB.

DVD-R. Stands for Digital Versatile Disc-Recordable. These discs can be burned once, and then played back in nearly any consumer DVD player and DVD capable computer. Use DVD-R (General) for your iDVD projects; DVD-R (Authoring) discs are not supported by iDVD.

DVD-ROM. Stands for Digital Versatile Disc-Read Only Memory. The format of a digital video disc that holds data which doesn't need to be played back automatically in a DVD player. Data can be stored but not altered in this format.

Effect. A special visual touch to enhance your movie. Choose from a variety of styles including Black & White, Earth-quake, and Fairy Dust—or layer them upon the same clip for snazzier results.

Encoding. In iDVD, the method by which your movie is compressed and formatted to fit onto a DVD disc. iDVD offers two types of encoding: Best Quality and Best Performance.

FireWire. A high-speed serial data bus that can move large amounts of data between computers and peripheral devices. Use a high-speed FireWire connection to import your footage from your camcorder into iMovie on your computer.

Footage. Movie clips, raw or edited; the stuff you download from your camcorder into iMovie and eventually turn into a finished project.

Frame. A single picture on a strip of film or video, or a single photo exposure.

Gigabyte (GB). A unit of computer data or storage space equivalent to 1,024 megabytes (MB).

iDVD Chapter Markers. Created in iMovie, these titled thumbnails indicate a new section that will appear as a separate section in iDVD. Clicking a chapter marker in iMovie also lets you jump to specific scenes in the film.

Import. Copying video and audio from your camera to your computer's hard disk, using a FireWire cable, iMovie, and a huge amount of hard disk space.

Jump cut. Hard, quick transition between clips.

Ken Burns Effect. A method of panning, zooming in, or zooming out on a still photo; named after the acclaimed documentary filmmaker who popularized the technique.

Liquid Timeline. Home of the Clip Viewer and Timeline Viewer, where all the movie-making editing occurs.

Map. In iDVD, the Map view illustrates the DVD project's content structure.

Media pane. Part of iDVD's Customize panel, the Media pane allows you to access other iLife-related content, such as photos, movies, and music.

Mode switch. Toggle between import mode (camera icon) and edit mode (scissors icon) using this small control above the Liquid Timeline.

Monitor. Preview and edit all your video clips—or play back your entire movie— on this large screen in iMovie.

Motion. Movement or animation, added to increase your DVD's coolness quotient.

Multiplexing. The process by which audio and video data are fused into one stream that DVD players can read.

Pane. An area containing goodies that can be added to create your movie, such as clips, photos, audio, titles, transitions, and effects.

Pane buttons. Displayed below iMovie's Shelf, these icons for Clips, Photos, Audio, Titles, Transitions, Effects and iDVD can be clicked to access all of the program's editing tools.

Playhead. Inverted triangle marker that appears on the Liquid Timeline and on the Monitor's Scrubber Bar. Drag the Playhead to any frame within your movie or clip to display it in the Monitor; the numbers beside the Playhead indicate the time location within the movie.

Preview. Just as it sounds, a preview is a chance to see how an edit or application affects your movie before you commit to accepting the change. In iDVD, click the Preview button to enter Preview mode and see what your project will look like when viewed on a DVD player.

QuickTime movie. QuickTime is a highly versatile format for sharing movies as files on your hard drive.

Rendering. The process of recreating clips in iMovie to incorporate new visual data such as transitions, titles, and effects.

Resolution. The amount of detail in an image, represented by pixels. For example, video resolution is typically more coarse than the resolution of a photo taken with a digital still camera.

Scrubber Bar. Scroll bar that allows you to move anywhere in a movie. Use the Monitor's Scrubber Bar to select a range of frames for copying, cutting, or cropping.

Settings pane. Part of iDVD's Customize panel, this pane lets you edit specific options such as text font and size, button styles, background images, and more.

Shelf. Also called the Clips pane, this display of video clips and photos appears next to the Monitor.

Slideshow. Just like Grandma and Grandpa's giant tray of vacation slides; but this one is created in iDVD by displaying pictures stored in iPhoto.

Split. To slice a clip where the Playhead is located; place the Playhead on the desired point in a clip and choosing Split Video Clip from the Edit menu.

glossary

Submenu. In iDVD, a submenu is a separate branch of the main menu, offering access to other media within your iDVD project (more movies or slideshows, for example). After creating an iDVD project from within iMovie, a button labeled Scene Selection is created; that button is actually a submenu (also known as a folder) that leads you to the chapters that comprise your movie.

Submenu theme. Visual flavor of the backdrop for your submenu. In this book's example, iDVD's Road Trip theme is selected for the submenu; the driver's perspective of the open highway serves as the backdrop for Jeff's Arizona 2004 chapter selections.

Theme. The overall look of a menu screen, including the visual presentation (fonts, colors, etc.) as well as the way it interacts (with motion menus, etc.).

Timecode. A method all camcorders use to label and keep track of footage, where time is shown as Hours: Minutes: Seconds: Frames. In video, 30 frames equal 1 second.

Timeline. The row beneath the Monitor where clips, photos, and transitions are arranged and edited. Also known as the Liquid Timeline, and made up of the Clip Viewer and Timeline Viewer.

Timeline Viewer. Arranges the clips in order and also depicts their lengths. This viewer also includes audio tracks and controls for changing aspects of a clip.

Title (iDVD). The name you choose for your movie, which is formatted differently than other buttons and elements in an iDVD theme. Edit the title's text and position in iDVD's Settings pane.

Title (iMovie). Any clip containing text that is superimposed over footage. Accessed by the Titles pane.

Transition. Stylish method for moving from one clip to the next. Access transitions including Fade In, Fade Out, Push or Twirl by selecting the Trans button just below the Shelf.

Trim. To shorten, as with a film clip. Also see Direct Trimming.

Waveforms (or, audio waveforms). Visual depiction of a clip's sound levels, that allows you to edit audio clips with more precision.

Zoom field. In iMovie's Photos pane, this is the field beside the Zoom slider. Change the duration of a zoom action by typing a value into this field.

Zooming in. In iMovie, zooming in refers to punching up the size of your various movie components for a better view. Zooming in is helpful when you're editing small clips or transitions.

Zoom slider. Bottom left-hand gauge that determines how much of the Timeline is shown in the viewer: with the slider at the left, the entire movie appears in the Timeline. In the Photos pane, the Zoom slider dictates how much of a photo is visible.

index

index

index

index

index

index

Ready to Learn More?

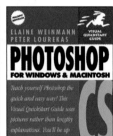

If you enjoyed this project and are ready to learn more, pick up a *Visual QuickStart Guide*, the best-selling, most affordable, most trusted, quick-reference series for computing.

With more than 5.5 million copies in print, *Visual QuickStart Guides* are the industry's best-selling series of affordable, quick-reference guides. This series from Peachpit Press includes more than 200 titles covering the leading applications for digital photography and illustration, digital video and sound editing, Web design and development, business productivity, graphic design, operating systems, and more. Best of all, these books respect your time and intelligence. With tons of well-chosen illustrations and practical, labor-saving tips, they'll have you up to speed on new software fast.

> " When you need to quickly learn to use a new application or new version of an application, you can't do better than the **Visual QuickStart Guides** from Peachpit Press."
>
> Jay Nelson
> *Design Tools Monthly*

www.peachpit.com